H They Stand

BIBLICAL SERMONS from EASTERN EUROPE

Compiled and Edited by
Lewis A. Drummond

JUDSON PRESS ® VALLEY FORGE

HERE THEY STAND

Copyright © Marshall, Morgan & Scott 1976
Published in the United States by Judson Press, Valley Forge, Pennsylvania 1978

ISBN: 0-8170-0790-3
Library of Congress Catalog Number: 77-92876

This book of sermons
from Preachers of the Gospel
is dedicated to:

J. I. (JIM) McCormick

A layman who has been
a true friend to preachers

Printed in the United States of America

Contents

	Page
Preface	v
Sermons from the Soviet Union	1
Michael Zidkof	
THE GREAT INVITATION OF CHRIST!	4
Benjamin Fedichkin	
SUFFERING FOR THE SALVATION OF OTHERS	13
Serzei Petrovich Fadiukin	
CONCERNING THE CHURCH	20
Walter Arthur Mitskevitch	
THE SIGNIFICANCE OF THE ASCENSION OF JESUS CHRIST	28
Sermons from East Germany	39
Hans-Gunther Sachse	
THE GIFTS AND THE BODY	42
Adolf Pohl	
PUT INTO PRACTICE WHAT YOU HAVE LEARNED	50
Fritz Petersen	
THE GOOD SHEPHERD	56
Wolfgang Klempert	
THE VICTORY GOD GIVES	66
Sermons from Romania	75
Petru Popovici	
THE WEAKNESSES OF MAN AND THE POWER OF THE ALMIGHTY GOD	78
THE TESTIMONY OF JESUS	85
Alexander G. Balc	
CONFRONTATION ON MOUNT CARMEL	96

Sermons from Hungary   103
Andreas Herjeczki
    THE THREE-FOLD WORK OF THE HOLY SPIRIT   107
Janos Hanyik
    THE OTHER VILLAGE   114

Sermons from Poland   119
Michael Stankiewicz
    IN THE FACE OF GUILT AND LOVE   122
    THE RE-CREATION OF THE INDIVIDUAL   129

Sermons from Yugoslavia   139
Josip Horak
    THE GREAT DISCOVERY OF A YOUNG MAN   142
Franjo Klem
    MARANATHA   150
    WHEN THE CRUMBS BECOME BIG LOAVES   153

Sermons from Bulgaria   159
Pastor Angeloff
    LONGING FOR HEAVEN   162
    ARISE YE, AND DEPART   166
    WHERE IS ZEBEDEE?   171

A Sermon from Czechoslovakia   177
Stanislav Svec
    ABIDE WITH US!   180

The Bible passages at the head of each sermon are from the Revised Standard Version Bible, and are used by permission.

Preface

Sermons from behind the iron curtain! Here is a most unusual compilation of messages from ministers of the gospel. They come from communist Europe, preached by men who know what it is to "stand fast in the Lord". They vibrate with courage, warmth and passion for the good news of Jesus Christ; that message which communicates to all men in all circumstances.

There is a two-fold purpose in presenting these messages to the West. First, the simple preaching of the gospel is always a source of blessing. This is especially true when it is preached in the context from which these sermons emerged. Therefore I trust these messages will help and encourage the reader.

Secondly, some in the West who are familiar with communist countries have made the innuendo that the pastors and churches which exist "above ground" in eastern Europe are not truly Christian or faithful to the gospel. These biblical sermons, which were actually preached in the eastern countries by faithful ministers in the churches, should once and forever dispel that myth. These men do preach the Word of God – and preach it in power and purity. Having myself visited and preached in many of these churches, I am thoroughly convinced of the genuineness of these men and churches. How grateful I am that the opportunity and privilege to do so was granted to me. I sincerely hope that the gospel purity that shines in and through the messages in this book will enlighten readers to the true situation.

Thus, these sermons are presented with the prayer that they will bless and enlighten all, and especially that they will motivate Christians to pray for and empathize with their brethren behind the iron curtain. If this happens, the volume will be well justified.

LEWIS A. DRUMMOND

Sermons from
THE
SOVIET UNION

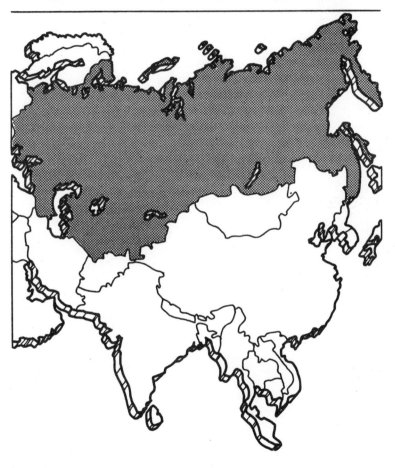

Michael Zidkof
Senior Pastor, Moscow Baptist Church

Michael Zidkof was born in 1928 in Leningrad, USSR, into the family of a Baptist preacher. In 1943 he joined the Church and sang in the choir of the Baptist Church in Moscow. He started preaching in 1955. From 1956 to 1958 he studied at Spurgeon's College in London, England, and again from 1961 till 1962 in MacMasters Theological College, Canada. In 1963 he was appointed second minister in the Moscow Baptist Church and in 1966 he became senior preacher in that church which now numbers 5,000 members in its congregation. From 1964 to 1969 he served on various committees of the European Baptist Federation. He led in the meetings of the Baptist Federation which took place in 1966. In 1969 he was a member of the Steering Committee of the Federation. He is an outstanding preacher and world leader in Baptist affairs.

The great invitation of Christ

Michael Zidkof

Matthew 11: 28–30

*Come to me, all who labour and are heavy laden,
and I will give you rest. Take my yoke upon you,
and learn from me; for I am gentle and lowly in
heart, and you will find rest for your souls. For
my yoke is easy, and my burden is light.*

In 1960 I had the privilege of participating as a delegate in the Baptist World Alliance Congress. We met in Brazil, in the beautiful city of Rio de Janeiro. This world renowned city is located on the coast of the Atlantic Ocean and is surrounded by towering mountains. One of the most striking things about the entire area is the "Christ of the Andes". On top of one of the peaks near Rio a majestic white statue of Christ has been erected, of such colossal dimensions that it can be seen from a great distance. It literally dominates the whole panorama. This Christ in stone stands with open arms looking down on the city in compassion.

This beautiful work of art presents to my mind something of a parable in marble for today. What I mean is, one must see not merely a majestic *image* of Christ, but the Lord Jesus Christ *Himself*, living and active and full of love and compassion, looking down, not just on Rio de Janeiro, but down on every city, valley and town in the world. There He must be seen with open arms, inviting all men to come to Him. And this can only mean that He is inviting you and me to come to Him to find that vital rest of soul which He alone can impart.

Now it is essential to understand that Jesus Christ, who invites us, is standing not far away from any of us. He knows all about our problems and weaknesses. Moreover, He knows those tremendous possibilities which have been implanted in us by the Eternal Creator. So in the midst of our perplexities, disappointments, worries and frustrations, Christ sees us in our weariness and has power to give us rest.

Christ and the Burden of Guilt

We all well know that today there are many frustrations and difficulties we must face. For example, there is the burden of an awakening conscience; the burden of the condemning voice of guilt. And when conscience starts to speak, it seems there is often little or nothing that can stop it. When some neighbour or friend tells us something unpleasant, we can ask him to stop or we can avoid meeting him. But how can we escape from ourselves? The condemning voice of conscience seemingly grows and grows.

History is full of illustrations of the power and torment which an awakened conscience brings to man. In the New Testament we have a perfect example in Judas Iscariot. He was a disciple of Jesus Christ. He actually walked with Jesus. Yet he betrayed his Master for thirty pieces of silver. But then his conscience began to speak. He realized his crime, as his own words reveal: "I have betrayed an innocent man to death." In a vain attempt to silence his conscience Judas gave back the money. But, alas! This did not help. The voice of conscience rang louder and louder until he could stand it no longer. So he took his life, to still the cries of his tormenting conscience.

O friends, even though all of your acquaintances tell you that you are a good man, if your own conscience says that you are guilty before men and before God, then all their comforting words mean nothing. When you know that you are not right before God, the voice of your conscience will increasingly make you aware of that fact. What are you to do? Where can you go to find relief? There is one place – and only one. *That is Golgotha.* There you will find One to whom you can go; the Lord Jesus Christ. Listen to the way He prayed for you: "Father! Forgive them." Oh, He is full of forgiveness. And His forgiveness has

5

the power to cleanse. He can truly give you that much desired peace. Listen to His words of invitation: "Come to me and I will give you rest." Come to me just as you are and I will receive you and give you forgiveness and renewal of life and the strength to start all over again. "Come now and let us reason together, saith the Lord. Though your sins be as scarlet they shall be as white as snow; though they be red like crimson, they shall be as wool." What marvellous promises! And these truths are not just smooth, soothing, unrealistic words. They are blessed *reality*.

A Personal Testimony

Many years ago I experienced the miracle and power of Christ's forgiveness. I was born and brought up in the family of a Baptist pastor, enjoying all of the benefits of having believing parents. When I became older I was enticed away from Christian principles. I began living in such a way that I was robbed of any true satisfaction and peace. Actually, I was living with a double standard. At home I feigned a Christian way of life. But outside of the home another kind of standard determined my life style. My parents, of course, knew my problem. They would invite me to attend their church. And for their sake I sometimes visited the services. Naturally, this course brought deep inner conflict. I tried to soothe my troubled conscience by rationalizing that I had Christian parents, sometimes went to church, sometimes read the Bible and sometimes prayed. What more did I have to do to be a Christian? I attempted to convince myself that this was enough. One day, however, we received a photograph of some of our relatives. On the back was written: "This picture was taken by a brother in Christ." Strange as it may seem, these simple words pierced my heart. A brother in Christ! This I could not say about myself. Day and weeks passed, and for me it became clear that having believing parents and attending church did not make me a true Christian. I found that I was guilty before God. I became conscious of the fact that I was a sinner.

Now I had seen people converted at our church services. I was amazed at the wonderful change these persons experienced. One such occasion particularly moved me. God spoke to me profoundly at that moment. I wanted to pray and to ask Him then and there to do the same for me, but shame and pride kept me back. I walked toward my home deeply disturbed, and there God arrested me. I stopped right on one of the wide Moscow streets; I could resist God no longer. Right there I prayed, asking the Lord to forgive me. And the miracle came! I personally experienced what it means to be forgiven by God. It was wonderful. He took away my burden of sin, giving me peace. I knew that I had been reconciled to God. Our Lord is such a marvellous Lord! He can always forgive.

My dear friend, won't you come to Him? You too can find this priceless peace with God. If you will simply seek God's forgiveness through our Lord Jesus Christ, you can experience the priceless gift of forgiveness of sins.

Christ and the Burden of Suffering

Then, there are today in many of our lives the burdens of illness, suffering, heartache, and so on. And these burdens are particularly heavy when we cannot see the way out. We all, quite naturally, want to be liberated from painful circumstances. We can all identify with the Psalmist when he said: "Oh that I had wings like a dove! For then would I fly away and be at rest . . . I would hasten my escape from the windy storm and tempest." (Psalm 55: 6, 8). But often there seems to be no escape, no way out.

Dear friend, are you going through sufferings and difficulties? Are you in the position of which the prophet Isaiah speaks: "O thou afflicted, tossed with tempest and not comforted"? Then listen to what the Lord Jesus says to you in such an hour: "Come to me and I will give you rest." Look at this promise! He does not say that He will *change* your difficulties and thus deliver you *from* the circumstances you are in. He speaks about something far greater than that. He wishes to give you His precious *peace* that you so desperately need in the *midst* of your difficulties. He gives rest to your soul in the face of your hardship.

Of course, circumstances influence a man. No one is totally unaffected by his environment. But in the final analysis, the main factor is not the circumstance, but our attitude towards it. An Arabian proverb says, "The same fire that melts the butter also makes an egg hard." The same difficulties and sufferings can harden a man or ennoble him. It all depends on how we relate

7

these trying times to our faith in Christ. Remember, "Come to me," our Lord invites, and "I will give you rest in your difficulties." The Lord promises to give us strength. We can become conquerors over all the difficulties of life. "In the world you will have trouble. But courage! The victory is mine. I have conquered the world." This is the word of our Lord, and it is not abstract theory or mere sentimental, comforting words. The power of God actually gives us strength in the moment of our need.

A Friend's Experience

An illustration of this marvellous truth is found in the life of one of my friends. He is now a man of thirty-five. When he was only seventeen he contracted an incurable illness which put him in bed permanently. He can now move only his hands and neck. You can imagine how great a burden of suffering he constantly bears. In his hours of severe pain he at first cursed his life. Then our believers started to visit him. They talked with him about God and His eternal power. And a miracle took place. This young man committed his life to Jesus Christ. In a moment he was transformed by the power of the Lord Jesus Christ. His circumstances have not been changed; he is still bedridden and in pain. But how different he is! He now knows Him who gives us strength to be a conqueror in our difficulties. He said to me one day: "How I would like to walk as all of you do! But my situation is still bearable, for I know about a neighbour who cannot even move his hands." Once I visited him with a relative of mine. Our visit was very short and afterwards my relative said to me, "I expected to see this young man depressed by his illness, but I was surprised to see him filled with the joy of living. And how his face shone!" Then he stopped and asked me, "Does this mean that faith helps?" Of course; it is the only hope! And the life of my friend proves it. Jesus gives peace in *all* difficulties.

Christ and the Burden of a Meaningless Life

Then there is a burden of a monotonous and meaningless life. So many experience this problem today. The twentieth century is an era of great change. It is an exciting time to live in. All the same, monotony and boredom seem to dominate many lives.

Every day the same unimportant duties demand our attention and time; at home, in the place of our work – even the life of the church seems dull at times. Oh, if we could only do a great heroic deed! Or, if we could but carry on a creative, important job! That would bring meaning to life, we feel. But every day the same routine goes on and on with no hope of change. What can one do to find zest in life? Do you ask these questions? Then listen; Christ says, "Come to Me. I will give you something very important. I will open your eyes and show you eternal meaning in these everyday duties." Paul said, "Whatever you are doing, put your whole heart into it, as if you were doing it for the Lord and not for men" (Col. 3:23). To serve God Himself – what greater honour could one ever hope to enjoy? That brings genuine meaning and reality to life.

So Christ is very near to you, and He puts meaning into every moment of every day if you will but let Him. He gives forgiveness and can make you a conqueror over any difficulty. He invites you to come to Him and to take that very important step to receive what He offers. He is offering you life in all its fullness. Do you hear His invitation? What is your reaction? He is still waiting for you. Come to Him, and you will find a life of abundant happiness.

Benjamin Fedichkin
Preacher, Moscow Baptist Church

*Benjamin Fedichkin was born into a Christian family.
His mother and father were members of an Evangelical
Christian Church in a rural area of Russia. His
grandparents were ministers of the Church in the
Smolensk province.*

*He came to know the teaching of Christ in very early
childhood but, as he states, "I understood it little, and
even less did I follow all that my parents taught me. Yet
at times I was ashamed of my bad behaviour."*

*In 1943, during the second world war, Benjamin
Fedichkin's mother became severely ill. These were
very difficult times. Famine was widespread. The doctors
did all that was possible to save her, but there was little
hope. At that time Benjamin was only twelve. He tells
of his mother's illness in this way: "My youngest sister
and I were, of course, deeply desirous that our mother
would live. Our grandmother, a very devout Christian,
told us that if we would beseech the Lord Jesus Christ
to spare our mother's life, He would answer us. And we
simply believed that. It was springtime. The forest had
turned a beautiful green. My sister and I went into
the forest, knelt, and prayed to God for a long time with
bitter tears. We begged Him for only one thing: 'Lord,'
we prayed, 'we have no father and our mother is on the
brink of death. We beseech thee, please restore our
mother's health.' I do not remember how long we stayed
on our knees, but I well remember that we got up and
ran to the hospital, feeling certain that she was getting
better. And so it was. Now I could thank the Lord that
he had heard my prayer. That same day I prayed once more.
In that prayer I also asked Him to forgive all
of my sins and to make me His worthy follower. While
I was praying I felt my heart filling with joy. When I had*

finished my prayer, I had the firm faith that Christ had
forgiven me. I truly rejoiced in it. I told my mother and
grandmother that God had forgiven me, that I now had
the happiness of being saved. And my mother's health
was also marvellously restored."

He was baptized in Moscow on June 21, 1954. Even
before he had received baptism by water he had begun
to sing in the choir in the Moscow church of the
Evangelical Christian-Baptists. In 1958 he was elected
as assistant pastor and that same year he began to preach
the gospel of Christ.

Pastor Fedichkin says that his "heart is still filled
with the joy of salvation," and he states, "I rejoice and
thank my Saviour for eternal life." His wife is also a
devout believer. She loves Jesus Christ and helps her
husband in his ministry in many different ways. They
have three children; two daughters and a son. The elder
daughter was baptized on May 25, 1970, and serves the
Moscow church as one of its organists. All of the
children love God and faithfully attend church and
serve the Lord. Benjamin Fedichkin states, "We all
thank our Lord that He loves us and rejoice that we
have the Lord Jesus as our personal Saviour."

Suffering for the salvation of others

Benjamin Fedichkin

Acts 16: 25–34

*But about midnight Paul and Silas were praying
and singing hymns to God, and the prisoners were
listening to them, and suddenly there was a great
earthquake, so that the foundations of the prison
were shaken; and immediately all the doors were
opened and every one's fetters were unfastened.
When the jailer woke and saw that the prison doors
were open, he drew his sword and was about to
kill himself, supposing that the prisoners had
escaped. But Paul cried with a loud voice, "Do not
harm yourself, for we are all here." And he called
for lights and rushed in, and trembling with fear
he fell down before Paul and Silas, and brought
them out and said, "Men, what must I do to be
saved?" And they said, "Believe in the Lord Jesus,
and you will be saved, you and your household."
And they spoke the word of the Lord to him and
to all that were in his house. And he took them the
same hour of the night, and washed their wounds,
and he was baptized at once, with all his family.
Then he brought them up into his house, and set
food before them; and he rejoiced with all his
household that he had believed in God.*

Dear brothers and sisters, the words of Holy Scripture that form
the text of this message paint a quite out-of-the-ordinary picture

for us. The scene is a prison in Philippi. Now the prisons of two thousand years ago were places of suffering and misery; a place where evil doers received just punishment for their crimes. But there was a startling contrast in this prison. Among the offenders of Roman law are two apostles – two servants of God – Paul and Silas, and they are praying to God, which is *very much* out-of-the-ordinary. Actually, this passage of Scripture tells us of a number of unusual occurrences which happened in this prison: there was triumphant singing in the dungeon, a devastating earthquake occurred, and one of the prisoners saved the prison keeper from suicide. Let us now look into this unusual drama in more depth.

Paul's Unusual Spirit

Paul and Silas were thrust into conditions in which the worst criminals of the Roman empire were herded. All through the long miserable night you could hear cursing, laments, groans and abuse. Naturally, it was very easy in such circumstances to join in with those who were lamenting their lot. Yet, right in the very midst of all this squalor, we hear something extraordinary; prayer and singing to the glory of God. Paul and Silas were raising their voices to God with thanksgiving. Continuing in prayer, they began to sing, praising the Creator of heaven and earth for His wonderful love to man; for His only begotten Son, the Saviour of the world.

Their, conduct was so unusual that the criminals who were there grew silent. Forgetting their circumstances and stopping their curses, they listened to the singing of these strange people. They listened to their prayers to the God who was unknown to the prisoners there.

You see, Paul and Silas believed in the power of Almighty God. They had given their hearts completely to Him and now they are fully trusting Him. In their prayers they give utterance to their hope and faith in God that their prayer will be answered. And praise God, their prayer was heard and God gave them a startling answer. Suddenly there was an earthquake. Could an earthquake be an answer to prayer? Yes, indeed it could!

This earthquake was of a most unusual nature. As a matter of fact, some theologians hold that this account in Acts 16 is an incorrect translation. They say the strange phenomenon was not

14

really an earthquake as no one suffered as a result of it. We must admit that normally an earthquake is a terrible disaster for any people. Sometimes they have cost thousands of human lives and the destruction of whole towns. We read, however, that as a result of *this* earthquake, "the doors were opened and everyone's bonds were loosed." No destruction in the usual sense at all! And it is the extraordinary nature of the earthquake that gives us the right to say that it was the answer to the prayer of God's servants.

Prison Doors Open

What power there must have been in Paul and Silas's prayers for God to answer them in this way! The doors were opened! The chains were loosed! O my dear friends, to see the doors of the prison opened – could there be anything more desirable in the life of anyone who finds himself in the same condition as Paul and Silas? Of course, there are always humanistic efforts to "open prison doors". The history of mankind abounds with human struggles to try to open the doors of prisons. But here the door opened itself! How? By the will and at the command of God!

Yes, the door was opened, and at the door stood the warden. What had occurred so frightened him that he was ready to put an end to his life. How does the apostle Paul react to this? At the very moment when freedom could be had through the open doors of the prison, is the apostle going to deny it to himself and to the rest? Paul could have let the prison keeper kill himself and then all could have left the dungeon.

Such moments in a man's life are extremely trying; when the fear of punishment pushes one to the edge of the chasm of sin. History records many instances when even Christians in such a position have failed. Some have taken up weapons at the moment of crisis; others have been merely passive, comforting themselves with the thought that they were not really responsible for the situation.

A Startling Act

But we read, "Paul cried out with a loud voice, 'Do yourself no harm, for we are all here.'" Even though Paul may well have suffered at the hands of this jailkeeper, we hear him giving his

15

answer to all who would reproach him for his action: "No, I do not need a freedom stained with blood. I can do without earthly blessings if having them would mean that the soul of an unrepentant sinner would perish eternally."

Surely that is why the apostle called out so loudly, "Do yourself no harm." How would those who were thirsting for freedom understand this? It sounds incredible that Paul would react as he did. Yet, having once placed his confidence in God, the apostle could no longer subject himself to the will of his own feelings. He must remain true to the spirit and mind of his Lord to the end. It was vital for Paul and Silas to show that it was a matter of first importance for them that not one soul should perish because of a selfish action on their part.

Little wonder that the keeper, grasping how extraordinary these men were, and recognizing them as God's own messengers, ran up to them and asked, "Sirs, what must I do to be saved?" There is life's ultimate question. "What must I do?" sobbed that soul. And what brought about that question? It was Paul, as the Lord's servant, showing such care and vital concern that the jailkeeper should not do away with himself!

Now this same question comes to Christians today – to believers in God all over the world. "What are we to do to be saved?" the sinners ask. And we must have an answer – and it must be backed up with the same vital concern shown by Paul and Silas.

A Life is Changed

When the warden turned to the apostle Paul, asking of him the way of salvation, Paul gave the simple answer: "Believe." That is the key. Faith in the Lord Jesus Christ secures forgiveness of sins and eternal life; a life liberated from the fear of death and punishment. And then, we read, "the jailkeeper washed their wounds and . . . when he had been baptized . . . prepared them a meal." Paul's deed in turning a man away from suicide to faith in Christ was rewarded and Paul was set free. Moreover, the man found peace with God and he devoted himself to the service of God and of his fellow men. All of this is implied in the beautiful account of the jailer's conversion. He was a transformed man.

Again, I ask, what was the secret of the whole affair? Paul was willing to display the spirit of Christ in the moment of his crisis. Able scholars of the word of God point to the similarity between the words of Paul, "Do yourself no harm", and the words of Christ uttered on the cross, "Father, forgive them for they know not what they do." It is a duty of the Christian not to seek his own privileges and welfare or easy paths through life, but to demonstrate selfless faithfulness so that he can show the true way to Christ. To point one to Calvary where Christ the crucified gives blessed forgiveness is life's greatest thrill. Our Lord always blesses His faithful ones with a reward for their labour of love and mercy. That is our task, for at the foot of the cross sinners find peace for their souls. There they receive forgiveness and eternal life and there everyone thirsting for salvation quenches his thirst. Therefore it is vital for us Christians to live in the spirit of Jesus so as to show the true way to Calvary, so that seekers on the way to God might never get lost because of our unfaithfulness; so that no one finds a stumbling block in us.

Thus may Christ teach us to observe all that He has commanded. May the Lord bless us all!

Serzei Petrovitch Fadiukin
Senior Pastor, Leningrad Baptist Church

Serzei Petrovich Fadiukin was born in Moscow on September 23, 1905 into a family of the working class. Until 1918 he resided in Moscow. Later, for a number of years, he lived in various districts of the USSR.

During his stay in the Semipalatinsk province, he met some Evangelical Christian-Baptists and in 1920 was converted to faith in Christ. The same year he was baptized and admitted into church membership. Soon afterwards he became a preacher of the gospel.

In 1922 he returned to Moscow. There he became a member of the great Moscow Baptist congregation. In 1924 he entered I. S. Prohanov's Biblical courses. In 1925 he married and the same year he became an ordained minister. From that time until now he has served the Baptist Union in Russia.

In the years 1960 to 1965 he served as a superintendent of the Evangelical Christian-Baptist congregation in Jahkent. Since 1967 he has been senior pastor and superintendent of the Leningrad Evangelical Christian-Baptist Church with 3,000 members.

Concerning the Church

Serzei Petrovitch Fadiukin

I Timothy 3:15

So that . . . you may know how one ought to behave in the household of God, which is the church of the living God, the pillar and bulwark of the truth.

In the brief words of our text, it has pleased the Holy Spirit to confront us through the apostle Paul with three great questions concerning the Church:
1) What is the Church?
2) What is the purpose of the Church?
3) How should we act as members of the Church?

First, may we consider: What is the Church?

It is vital to recognize at the very outset that the Church is the *Body of Christ* in which the Spirit of God lives. This is a tremendous thought. It immediately implies that members who are added to the Church body by our Lord are actually parts of His own Body. Therefore, they are united with all believers and are rooted and grafted into the heavenly olive tree by the indwelling of the Holy Spirit. Thus, becoming a part of the body, they can claim all of God's promises which He has given to His people. Possessing a living faith and being full of devotion to the sanctifying and purifying will and word of the Lord, there is formed a union between God and men that provides complete assurance in God's keeping presence and power. By being members of a body with its diverse, yet united, parts, they join and unite into the one organism with one soul and one heart under one Head: the Lord Jesus Christ. So the Church, as is the case with a body through its ligaments and sinews, must be governed by and united in Christ if it is to grow in the divine manner (see Col. 2: 19). Everyone in the body, binding himself to God by faith, becomes free from the power of sin and thus able to be built up through love (see Eph. 4: 16).

Some Important Truths

Now some conclusions must be drawn from this principle. First, the Church of Christ (irrespective of its man-given name) is a society of the believers into which *only* redeemed people should be accepted. During our Lord's ministry on earth such persons as Nicodemus, a teacher of the Israelite people; Joseph of Arimathea, a member of the council; the wife of Chuza, Herod's manager; and others like Zacchaeus, Mary of Magdala, etc., were those who made up the body of disciples (Luke 8: 3; 23: 50–53; John 19: 38–42). And all of them represented the society of the believers. This principle is foundational to the entire system. Therefore, when we ask who should be a church member, the answer is obvious; only genuine believers should become members of a local congregation.

Secondly, the Church *belongs* to the living God (1 Tim. 3: 15), for He purchased it at the cost of His own blood (Acts 20: 28). So in the active, corporate life of the Church, there is but one authority; the Lord Jesus Christ. "For there is but one God, and one intermediary between God and men – the man Christ Jesus, who gave himself as a ransom for all men" (1 Tim. 2: 5–6). Hence, one can confidently conclude that the universal principles upon which the Church is based come from Christ Himself. And these principles are accepted on the basis of Christ's Lordship. Therefore, they demand from those who accept them submission, that is, submission to Christ's own heavenly and charitable influence. Moreover, it must be emphasized that there is no human intermediary between God and man. Christ alone fills that position.

Now the Lord Jesus Christ, through His eternal Word, established His order and practice for the Church, viz., solemnity, decency in the visible worship, and simplicity for the understanding of His truth (1 Cor. 14: 32–33).

Furthermore, Christ intends His church to be an indissoluble

21

spiritual unity (without visible links). As John said, "If we walk in the light . . . we have fellowship with one another" (1 John 1: 7).

To implement these foundational principles in the life and worship of the Body, Christ imparted the leadership and influence of His Holy Spirit and gave the gift of His beneficial Word. Thus through constant prayer and intercession with our Head, the Church lives out its life in chaste and pure behaviour in all places and under all conditions. This now leads to our next inquiry.

Our second question is: What is the purpose of the Church?

Quite naturally, when one attempts to define the purpose of the Church, one is almost at a loss. God's purpose for His Church is multiple. It is His arm of might in the world, it is the agent of evangelism, etc. – the list could be expanded almost endlessly. But one important aspect of the Church's purpose is found in the fact that the Body of Christ is to be the pillar and foundation of divine truth. As a massive pillar or column supports the capital of a building, the Church is straight, unchangeable and constant in its support of the truth of God. Let us look at this one aspect of the Church's purpose for being. In an age of conflicting concepts, this phase of the Church's ministry is most relevant.

The Importance of Truth

The Church's stance on truth is vital in all ages and cultures, for those who depend on their own mental and rational abilities alone to discover truth, the truth can often be distorted and corrupted. As a classic example, there were in the Antioch church in the times of the apostle Paul some professing believers who had come from Jerusalem raising the question as to whether the grace of Christ alone was sufficient to save (Acts 15). They advocated that keeping some of the Mosaic law was necessary in order to be rightly related to God. This, of course, deeply disturbed many of the church members in Antioch. This teaching was certainly different from the gospel they had heard from Paul. A conference was called in Jerusalem to consider the matter. And the decision of the apostles and the elders, jointly with the

22

church in Jerusalem, put an end to all the disagreements and disturbing elements stirred up by "dishonourable zealots," who knew "neither the Scriptures nor the power of God". The Church stood for the truth – and the problem was resolved.

Of course, it is human nature to err. Even church members can fall into serious error. Thus a strong bulwark against error must be raised. And God has provided for this need through His Church. The Church is the main repository of his revelation. So if a man begins to isolate himself from the Church, think of himself as the only reservoir and pillar of truth, thus opposing the authority of the Church as a whole, that man can easily fall into the same trap as did the Judaizers of Paul's day. It is the Church as a Body to whom God has entrusted His Word. To separate ourselves from it and to become a law unto ourselves is to court error and judgment.

This leads us finally to consider: How should we act as members of the Church?

Christ said in His high priestly prayer, "I do not ask you to take them out of the world, but to keep them from the evil one" (John 17: 15). Our Lord does not envision His Church separated and isolated from the surrounding cultural conditions of its age. Actually, He sent the Church into the world as the "salt of the earth" so that it could fulfill its purpose of declaring God's truth. Therefore, the Church must be vitally alive to the sociological and cultural milieu in which it finds itself, if it is to minister effectively.

A well-known Baptist thinker, Professor Walter Rauschenbusch, said in a speech entitled "Social Crisis and the Church" delivered at the World Baptist Congress in Philadelphia, 1911: "The Church is deeply involved in the social crisis. She has a sacred duty, for which she is responsible to God and nations." Now if the Church keeps herself from social involvement because of her shyness and conservatism, she hands over many great issues to other leaders. If the Church resists or ignores movements for justice and equality, she helps to create grief and anarchy, and excites hatred against religion. This raises the question as to how the Church and her members can take part in the solution of vital questions. In what way can we exercise a beneficial influence and thus fulfill our ministry as the Church of Jesus Christ?

Take, for example, the dilemmas, strife and mistrust in all segments of societies and nations. The burden of responsibility is on those who really love our Lord Jesus Christ; on all who want to see His ideals realized. We must take seriously the words of our Lord when He said, "Blessed are the peacemakers, for they will be called sons of God." The Church, like flashing lightning, must help to dispel the darkness of fear, anxiety and distrust that breeds misunderstanding and strife. Therefore, *every church member* – the father, the husband, the son, the mother, and daughter – whether one has great or little influence in the family or community; every Christian must give himself to all ennobling efforts. To express it personally, do you contribute by your influence to the purpose of Christ in this world? Do you manifest the love of Christ to all people and love all people in His name? Is the influence you have directed to the honour of Jesus Christ and the happiness of men? We can do this by seeing "that we are above reproach in the eyes of everyone" (Rom. 12: 17). And then because of our purpose in the world, we must in every possible way encourage and as far as possible carry into all of life that which is good and true and that which guards our neighbours against injustice and wrong.

In other words, the ultimate question is: how do you act in relationship to other people? All around there are people for whom you can dispel fear and help meet their needs and thus become a point of blessing in the name of Jesus Christ. Brothers and sisters, wherever we live, whatever language we speak, as church members we must thrust ourselves into relevant issues. The gospel of Christ is dependent upon our involvement in the lives of people.

Little Issues Are Important Too

But along with these issues, the Church has other problems – problems concerning *individual* members of the Church. These issues are daily encountered in the routine of life. It is true that these issues are on a limited scale, but in spite of their limitation, they are often as important as the so-called "larger" issues. For example, in Paul's letter to Timothy, the Apostle wrote, "But set those who believe an example in speech" (1

24

Tim. 4: 12). Everyone in the Church ought to know how to speak as becoming a Christian.

The issue on this point is: our words betray our real selves. For example, is there in your words a striving for self exaltation? Or do you use your speech to impose your will on others? On one occasion the apostle said to the Corinthians, "For Jews insist upon miracles, and Greeks demand philosophy, but we proclaim a Christ who was crucified – an idea that is revolting to Jews and absurd to the heathen, but to those whom God has called, whether they are Jews or Greeks, a Christ who is God's power and God's wisdom" (1 Cor. 1: 22–26). You see, our words should speak of Jesus Christ. Of course, this can be costly. Perhaps we may even experience persecution and be made subject to reproaches and censures because of abandoning our speech to Jesus Christ. But we must yield our tongues to Jesus. And a real part of that means we shall declare and live out His truth fully and faithfully.

Paul writes: "For I am not a peddler of (I do not distort, do not insert my own ideas in) God's message, like most men, but like a man of sincerity (without any ambiguity), commissioned by God (without any human fiction), and in his presence (i.e., with reverence), in union with Christ I utter His message (that is, in the strength of grace and love)" (2 Cor. 2: 17). That is the principle we must have deeply ingrained into our entire life.

The old lesson of Scripture is always applicable: "Never go beyond the letter" (1 Cor. 4: 6). All of life must be kept in the bounds and context of God's Word. What I am trying to say is simply this: Christians ought to set an example of Christ in the *entirety* of their lives.

We must never forget that our words, our actions, our lives – sometimes in very small details – are subject to severe scrutiny by unbelievers. They weigh and judge all we do. This is why Paul said, "I refuse to practice cunning or to tamper with God's message. It is by the open statement of the truth that I would commend myself to every human conscience in the sight of God" (2 Cor. 4: 2). "You will testify, and God will, how pure and upright and irreproachable our relations were with you who believed. You know how, like a father with his children, we used to urge, encourage, and implore you to make your lives worthy of God who invites you into his kingdom and his glory"

(1 Thess. 2: 10–12).

It is clear from these passages that words and actions are bound together. Our behaviour confirms the words of our witness. Therefore, there must never be a gap or a dissonance between the witness and the life of the believer. Godly living must back up our proclaiming of the gospel. The apostle writes for all of us when he says, "so that the lives we live may be worthy of our Master and wholly pleasing to him." Moreover, he writes these words of admonition so that we may be fruitful in all kinds of effective good deeds and may grow into a fuller knowledge of God.

And when we live like this, His mighty power will strengthen us with perfect strength for the cheerful exercise of endurance and forbearance in every situation; and you will thank the Father who has entitled you to share the lot of God's people in the realm of light. Never forget, He has rescued us from the dominion of darkness, and has transferred us into the realm of His dear Son, by whom we have been ransomed from captivity through having our sins forgiven. He, the Lord Jesus Christ, is the likeness of the unseen God, "for it was through him that everything was created in heaven and on earth, the seen and the unseen, angelic thrones, dominions, principalities, authorities – all things were created through him and for him. He existed before all things and he sustains and embraces them all. He is the head of the church, it is his body" (Col. 1: 10–18). Thanks be to God for His unspeakable gift. Therefore, let us live for Him in the fellowship of His glorious Church to the praise of His honour and glory.

Walter Arthur Mitskevitch
Preacher, Moscow Baptist Church

*Three generations of the Mitskevitch family have been
associated with the Evangelical Christian (Brethren) and
Baptist movements in Russia. Walter Mitskevitch's
father, the Reverend Arthur Mitskevitch, is now a
treasurer and a deputy General Secretary of the
All-Union Council of Evangelical Christian-Baptists of
the USSR.*

*Walter was educated as a dental surgeon and worked
as a dentist for twelve years. He was converted in 1955
and began to preach in a small church near Odessa,
Ukraine. That same year he was baptized in the Black
Sea. In 1964 he was elected a preacher of the Moscow
Evangelical Christian-Baptist Church. In 1966 he left
his dentistry and went to work in the office of the
Evangelical Christian-Baptists in the USSR. He has
worked in the secretarial department and with the newly
organized Bible correspondence courses. He was a
student of Spurgeon's College in London from 1970 to
1972.*

*Walter Mitskevitch is married; his wife is a medical
doctor. While Walter was in England she was elected a
preacher of the Moscow Baptist Church. They have a
son and a daughter.*

The significance of the ascension of Jesus Christ

Walter Arthur Mitskevitch

Acts 1: 1–14

In the first book, O Theophilus, I have dealt with all that Jesus began to do and teach, until the day when he was taken up, after he had given commandment through the Holy Spirit to the apostles whom he had chosen. To them he presented himself alive after his passion by many proofs, appearing to them during forty days, and speaking of the kingdom of God. And while staying with them he charged them not to depart from Jerusalem, but to wait for the promise of the Father, which, he said, "you heard from me, for John baptized with water, but before many days you shall be baptized with the Holy Spirit."

So when they had come together, they asked him, "Lord, will you at this time restore the kingdom to Israel?" He said to them, "It is not for you to know times or seasons which the Father has fixed by his own authority. But you shall receive power when the Holy Spirit has come upon you; and you shall be my witnesses in Jerusalem and in all Judea and Samaria and to the end of the earth." And when he said this, as they were looking on, he was lifted up, and a cloud took him out of their sight. And while they were gazing into heaven as he went, behold, two men stood by them in white robes, and said, "Men of Galilee, why do you stand looking

28

into heaven? This Jesus, who was taken up from
you into heaven, will come in the same way as you
saw him go into heaven."

Then they returned to Jerusalem from the
mount called Olivet, which is near Jerusalem, a
sabbath day's journey away and when they had
entered, they went up to the upper room, where
they were staying, Peter and John and James and
Andrew, Philip and Thomas, Bartholomew and
Matthew, James the son of Alphaeus and Simon the
Zealot and Judas the son of James. All these with
one accord devoted themselves to prayer, together
with the women and Mary the mother of Jesus,
and with his brothers.

The Ascension was and is a great triumph of our Lord Jesus
Christ! Therefore, on Ascension Day the Evangelical Christian-
Baptist Churches as well as the Orthodox and other churches in
the Soviet Union have special morning and evening services. It
is somewhat sad that many churches in the West do not celebrate
this Christian festival. For many Christian people Ascension Day
passes quite unnoticed. This is something of a mistake in my
view. For Ascension Day presents an opportunity for believers
to hear again about one of the great events in the earthly life of
our Lord. Of course, all true Christians are happy to meditate
upon Christ's birth, His death, and His resurrection. But perhaps we should give more attention to His *ascension*. All of these
events are part of our Lord's wonderful life on the earth and the
Ascension becomes the logical conclusion of His work of pro-
viding salvation for all.

The Old Testament prophets predicted the ascension of the
Lord Jesus into heaven. We can read about this in many of the
psalms and prophetic books (Ps. 16: 8–11; 24: 7–10; 68: 18–20;
110: 1; 132: 11; Isa. 52: 13–15). Moreover, authors of various
books of the New Testament clearly paid considerable attention
to this remarkable event (Acts 2: 33; Eph. 1: 20–21; 4: 8; Heb.
1: 13; 8: 1, 9: 12; 10: 12; 1 Pet. 3: 22). The Ascension narrative is
presented to us by Luke the evangelist and historian in both of

his books. In the Gospel it forms the conclusion (Luke 24: 50–51) and in the Acts it stands as the beginning (Acts 1: 2, 6–9). And, of course, Jesus Christ Himself spoke about His leaving and exaltation into heaven (John 14–16, Luke 19: 11ff., etc.).

All this emphasis points up to the fact that the ascension of Jesus Christ has great significance for all of us. My sermon "The Significance of the Ascension of Jesus" has three main points to make:
1. The ascension of Christ (Acts 1: 9)
2. The last great promise of the ascending Christ (Acts 1: 5–8)
3. The last great commission of our ascended Lord (Acts 1: 8)

1. Let us look first at the ascension of Christ into heaven.

In the Acts of the Apostles, we read: "And when he had said this, as they were looking on, he was lifted up, and a cloud took him out of their sight" (Acts 1: 9).

When Jesus was taken up into heaven, only forty days had elapsed since He had been lifted upon the shameful wooden cross of Calvary. His body had been broken and beaten; the terrible crown of thorns had been pressed into His brow; the nails had pierced and torn His hands and feet; a piercing wound had been made in His side. In wounds and blood, in suffering and agony, *He died.* Some of His disciples were witnesses of that terrible death.

He was buried, but . . . in three days time Jesus Christ was gloriously raised from the dead by the power of God. Hallelujah! What a Saviour!

> I know that my Redeemer lives
> What joy the blest assurance gives!
> He lives, He lives, who once was dead;
> He lives, my everlasting Head!

These words of the hymn express the truth of the Resurrection. And what a great truth it is! Moreover, we read that our Lord Jesus Christ "presented himself alive, after his passion by many proofs, appearing to them during forty days, and speaking of the kingdom of God" (Acts 1: 3). What blessed meetings the risen Lord Jesus Christ must have had with His disciples!

Now, on what we call Ascension Day, Jesus Christ again met with His followers. They had gathered for that meeting on

Mount Olivet, not far from Bethany. They were a happy company. The disciples were very glad to have their Lord and Teacher among them; not only alive, but now resurrected and surrounded with mysterious glory which no one could again destroy.

The Saviour stood in the centre of the group and gave to His disciples His last instructions and promises. Then He lifted His pierced hands, and while He was pronouncing words of blessing, He began to rise from the earth. To their great astonishment He rose up above them "and a cloud took him out of their sight." Jesus Christ ascended into heaven to sit on the throne of power – on the right hand of God. This confirmed Christ's exaltation, finally and for all time.

He Ascended As Saviour

In the Russian city of Leningrad, where I was converted, there is the magnificent St Isaak's Cathedral. I personally think it is the most beautiful cathedral in the Soviet Union. In its main window one can see a large stained glass picture of the ascending Christ. It is breath-taking! Christ's robe is purple, as a king's mantle should be. But His marvellous face has the marks from the crown of thorns. There are nail prints on His hands and feet. These marks signify that as He went into heaven, He went as our Saviour; the Redeemer of sinners.

The Book of Revelation tells us that He is glorified in heaven as a *slain Lamb* (5: 6ff.). The author of the Letter to the Hebrews described His saving ministry as a priestly ministry. In Old Testament times, the priests sanctified the people through the sacrifice of animals. These liturgies were a prototype of our Lord's ministry. For He offered Himself as a holy, perfect sacrifice, once and for all, and "entered not into a sanctuary made with hands . . . but into heaven itself" (Heb. 9: 24). He thus became *our High Priest.* Therefore, He is the *Advocate and Intercessor* before God on behalf of sinners (Heb. 7: 25). By His sacrifice He took away human sin and opened the gates of eternity, the gates of paradise and heaven.

He entered into heaven as our *Friend;* as our *Helper* in temptation who sympathizes with our weaknesses and is ready to give help in time of need (Heb. 4: 15ff.).

31

How good it is to have such a Lord in heaven!

He went into heaven as the *Conqueror of death and hell*; as the *Lord of life and resurrection*. He who believes in Him has eternal life, he does not come into judgement, but has passed from death to life (John 5:24).

Jesus Is Lord

Now we can also clearly see that the Ascension revealed the *omnipotent sovereignty* of Jesus. Ten days after the Ascension, on the day of Pentecost, Peter the Apostle said, "This Jesus God raised up, and of that we all are witnesses. Being therefore exalted at the right hand of God, and having received from the Father the promise of the Holy Spirit, He has poured out this, which you see and hear. For David did not ascend into the heavens; but he himself says, 'The Lord said to my Lord, sit at my right hand, till I make thy enemies a stool for thy feet'" (Acts 2:32ff.). These words "at the right hand of God" were translated from Greek into Russian with the word *odesnuyu*. It shows the unity of Christ and the Godhead. It is a place of great authority.

The apostle Paul wrote about Christ's authority in his Letter to the Ephesians, chapter 1, verse 21ff: "God raised Christ from the dead and made him sit at his right hand in the heavenly places, far above all rule and authority and power and dominion, and above every name that is named, not only in this age, but also in that which is to come; and he has put all things under his feet and has made him the head over all things for the church . . ."

So we can conclude that Christ is indeed the King of kings and the Lord of lords. He has all authority in heaven and on earth. Crucified in weakness, Christ has ascended in power. Though lifted upon the shameful cross, He has been exalted in the place of everlasting glory and praise. Even though He suffered unto death, He was crowned with honour and sovereignty. Yes, He was rejected by Israel, but He was received by God; and now He lives forever.

How many lessons there are in the ascension of Jesus Christ! His kingship demands our obedience; we must respect His commandments in our daily lives. His sovereignty calls us to be His

32

faithful servants; His slaves to fulfill His will. And Jesus gave His commission to His disciples just before the Ascension; we are to be His witnesses in all the world. Moreover, He promised the necessary power and His presence to fulfill it.

2. So we now look at the last promise of Jesus Christ.

The Ascension ended the visible ministry of Jesus Christ on earth. And with this act His spiritual ministry began. On the Mount of Olives, at His ascension, Jesus charged His disciples "not to depart from Jerusalem, but to wait for the promise of the Father, which, he said, you heard from me, for John baptized with water, but before many days you shall be baptized with the Holy Spirit . . . You shall receive power when the Holy Spirit has come upon you" (Acts 1: 4–5, 8).

These words comprise one of the greatest promises of our ascended Lord. He promised the gift of the Holy Spirit. He promised to send the Holy Spirit of power into the hearts of the disciples. This blessed Spirit would descend from the Father; from heaven, that very place to which He, the Lord Jesus, ascended. And we know the Holy Spirit came upon the disciples. We read about this in the Acts of the Apostles in chapter 2, where we have a graphic account of the Day of Pentecost. The power of the Holy Spirit was manifested mightily on that day.

The Power of the Spirit Is Ours

There are many different aspects of power in this world. There is the power of nature, the power of wind and rivers, the power of electricity and atoms, the power of growing seeds and plants, etc. We know the power of physically strong men. We know the power of authority and knowledge. There are good and evil powers in the world, of many types and varieties. But the Holy Spirit is a *spiritual* and *personal* power. The Holy Spirit is God's Spirit. And He comes to bestow different gifts and nurture His fruit in regard to all of God's people.

How did the disciples receive the power of the Holy Spirit?

1. First, they *waited for it*. They knew God's promise, and they wanted God's power above all. The disciples waited in unity; they were *all together* in the upper room. They obeyed their

Lord. They did not try to force the hand of God. They were not impatient; they waited with deep faith in the promise of God. And they were blessed because of their patient trust.

2. Secondly, the disciples *prayed* for the promised power of the Holy Spirit: "All these with one accord devoted themselves to prayer" (Acts 1: 14). They prayed as their Lord taught them (Luke 11: 9–13). They prayed with all their soul, mind and strength. They prayed constantly and thus they received the answer.

3. Thirdly, they *recognized that this power was promised to them for the sole purpose of doing the work of God.* The disciples did not receive the power of the Spirit for themselves alone, but for a special task; to be witnesses of Christ in the world.

Yes, the disciples received this wonderful power of the Holy Spirit. God kept His word. And now *all* of Christ's disciples can have this great power for Christian life and ministry.

Of course, Jesus showed the great significance of His departure into heaven as it related to the receiving of the Holy Spirit. He said to his disciples, "I tell you the truth: it is to your advantage that I go away, for if I do not go away, the Counsellor will not come to you; but if I go, I will send him to you" (John 16: 7.). This implies two important points. First, the true Son of Man – God in human flesh – had some limitations as a man. In his flesh, he could not reveal in fullness all of the attributes of the divine Godhead. This was because of the limitations of His material body. He needed food and rest, He was limited in time and space, etc.

Secondly, the Holy Spirit was not to minister in fullness with the believers and towards the world until the Son returned to the Father. His work on the cross, His resurrection and ascension must be completed first. The Holy Spirit could enter into hearts of men only when they were cleansed by the blood of the ascended Lord Jesus Christ.

Now, the Holy Spirit is actually the Spirit of the ascended Christ. And His indwelling the hearts of the disciples shows the depth of the new, dynamic relationship between Christ and His followers (John 14: 18–20; Matt. 28: 20). This new relationship, based on completed salvation, brings great advantages and blessings to all disciples – and to the world, for that matter. For everyone is called to receive this new and wonderful fellowship with Jesus Christ through accepting Him as his personal Saviour.

34

Yes, we live every day in the light of the ascension of our Lord through the fellowship of the Holy Spirit; the Spirit of our Lord Jesus Christ. He comes into our hearts on the day when we repent and give our lives to the Lord. Thus, He dwells within the child of God and fills the Christian with Himself again and again for witnessing to Jesus Christ.

3. In the third and final place, let us consider the last commission of Jesus Christ.

One of the basic facts we see in the ascension of our Lord Jesus Christ is that after He finished His earthly ministry He commissioned His disciples to continue His work; to spread the good news of salvation everywhere. He promised His constant spiritual presence and power. The risen Christ sent His disciples to all nations and promised to be with them "always, to the close of the age" (Matt. 28: 19–20).

On Ascension Day He repeated His commission with the words: "and you shall be my *witnesses* in Jerusalem and in all Judea and in Samaria and to the end of the earth" (Acts 1: 8). He spoke prophetically and expressed His will. Ten days later His prophetic word was fulfilled.

The Spirit of God developed a great desire in the hearts of the disciples to bear witness of Christ to all people. Look at Peter on the Day of Pentecost. This same Peter who had denied that he was a disciple of Jesus of Nazareth now boldly preached the message of Jesus with great power before a whole multitude of people, and three thousand souls repented and were saved.

The Spirit of Christ transformed these simple men of Galilee – mere peasants – into great evangelists of the kingdom of God, and they spread the Good News into all the world. Actually, Christians witnessed to the whole pagan world. From Jerusalem the gospel reached to the ends of the earth.

There is an old Russian legend which states that Andrew the apostle spread the gospel in the Caucasus – in the south of my country. He is said to have preached also in the Greek colonies on the shore of the Black Sea. As a result of this – or at least of some faithful witnesses – I was baptized at the same place in the Black Sea some years later; nineteen hundred years later, in fact.

35

Throughout the world, in my country as well as in yours, the Christian witness is not in vain. And there is great joy in heaven and in the Church when many sinners repent and are converted. They receive the Holy Spirit into their hearts (John 14:17) and the Holy Spirit always develops in them a great desire to save other sinners. He makes them "fishers of men", as Jesus said. There are many examples of this. I shall tell you one.

In 1855, during the Crimean War an officer of the English army gave his heart to the Lord. His life was changed completely. He devoted his life to the great missionary enterprise. After 1873 he visited Russia many times. He came not as a soldier with sword, but as a missionary with the Bible and a powerful witness for Christ. His name was Lord Radstock. Many people were converted through his preaching in St Petersburg (Leningrad) the capital of Russia. Through that revival my grandparents became Evangelical Christian-Baptists. How I thank God for that! And many similar accounts could be given.

But here is the point, dear friends in Christ: "You shall be My witness," the Saviour said. This was His last commission to His disciples. And He confirmed His will by His glorious ascension. And this means that every true Christian should witness personally for his Lord. As true disciples, so we must be true witnesses to the risen, ascended Christ. "Here I stand," said Charles H. Spurgeon the great English preacher, "myself a proof of what the Lord can do. I am His servant, saved by Him and washed in His blood. I am, while I live, whether I speak or not, a witness of His love – a trophy of His grace." That is the true spirit of the faithful Christian disciple.

The Power of a Changed Life

Of course, there are a variety of ways to witness effectually. If we read the Acts of the Apostles we can see how many different ways there are of witnessing. But the important aspect of witnessing is the witness of a consistent Christian life. Every kind of witnessing is successful if it proceeds from a Christ-like life. The most powerful testimony is the testimony of a changed life. The world is weary with mere words. The greatest proof to the world of the risen, ascended Christ is a faithful Christian; one in whom Christ truly lives and through whom His life is flowing. This is a way in which every Christian can witness for the Lord. Yes, the witness of a transformed life has great power. Look at the life of the apostle Paul.

At the same time, however, every Christian should be ready to witness for the Lord by his words. It may be preaching to the crowd; or "preaching" to one person on a desert road, as Philip did (Acts 8: 35). The Spirit of Christ helps us in these ventures, for He gives understanding of God's Word and brings to our remembrance all that God has said (John 14: 26). Therefore, we can proclaim the great love of God in Jesus Christ. The Apostle Paul calls us to preach Christ crucified and ascended.

We are to be witnesses of what Jesus Christ has done. If we have met Christ, if we believe in Christ, let us tell others about Him. If we have a close fellowship with him, we have much to proclaim. We must witness to what we have experienced concerning Jesus Christ, to His transforming work within our hearts and character. We can witness through our written words in letters and books, through the hospitality of our homes and fellowship with needy people, through our money and possessions, through our whole life, day by day. We can find countless ways to be witnesses for our Lord in this world.

Jesus Christ provided salvation for the entire world. But this salvation can reach sinners only through redeemed people. The Lord makes His disciples fishers of men. He equips them with everything for this sacred work. It is, therefore, the responsibility of every Christian. In this sense, the salvation of souls depends on our obedience and faithfulness.

Yes, our Lord Jesus Christ ascended into heaven, but He always abides within us spiritually. He promised, and so gives, power to us to be His witnesses everywhere. May we all join in that great work for our ascended Lord and bring glory to His name! Amen.

Sermons from
EAST GERMANY

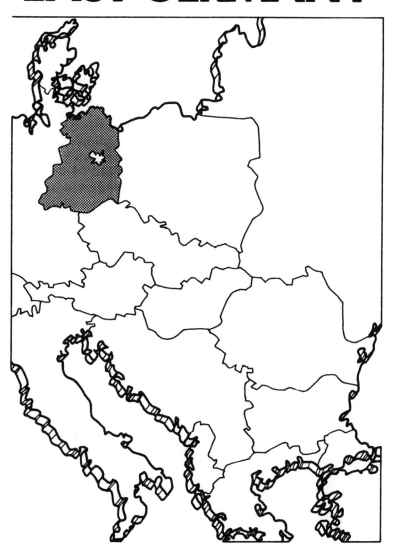

Hans-Gunther Sachse

The Reverend Hans-Gunther Sachse studied for the ministry from 1952 to 1956 at the Baptist Theological Seminaries at Hamburg and Rüschlikon. Thereafter he served as pastor of the Baptist churches at Mühlhausen and Stralsund. In 1969 he became pastor of the Baptist Church at Luckenwalde near East Berlin. Since 1975 he has served a church in East Berlin. He is married and has four children. He is a member of several committees for evangelism in his country and has taken an active part in denomination life.

The Gifts and the Body

Hans-Gunther Sachse

1 Corinthians 12:4–13

*Now there are varieties of gifts, but the same
Spirit; and there are varieties of service, but the
same Lord; and there are varieties of working, but
it is the same God who inspires them all in every
one. To each is given the manifestation of the Spirit
for the common good. To one is given through the
Spirit the utterance of wisdom, and to another the
utterance of knowledge according to the same Spirit,
to another faith by the same Spirit, to another gifts
of healing by the one Spirit, to another the working
of miracles, to another prophecy, to another
the ability to distinguish between spirits, to
another various kinds of tongues, to another the
interpretation of tongues. All these are inspired by
one and the same Spirit, who apportions to each
one individually as he wills.*

*For just as the body is one and has many
members, and all the members of the body, though
many, are one body, so it is with Christ. For by
one Spirit we were all baptized into one body –
Jews or Greeks, slaves or free – and all were made
to drink of one Spirit.*

On April 9, 1945, Dietrich Bonhoeffer, the famous German
pastor and theologian, was executed by the SS in a Nazi concentration camp. From this Christian martyr comes the statement: "A church which permits to stay within its fellowship
idle members who have no tasks [German: *welche nicht genutzt
werden*] will be reduced to ruin by these very members." Clearly

there are many such "idle" members in our churches today. Many of them obviously prefer this mere passive membership, even though they may seem to be attentive hearers and are viewed by those outside of the church as confessors of the Christian faith. And all churches seem to suffer from this situation. Thus a small ministerial group, for all practical purposes, does almost all the work in the church while most of the members remain virtually completely passive.

Now it is obvious that throughout church history the various truths and concepts in the Bible have not been presented at all times with equal clarity. This is true in our personal Bible study as well as with the corporate teaching of the Church. Then suddenly, quite unexpected, we rediscover a truth which has been neglected for possibly a long time. It may be a truth which was obscure for centuries. For example, Martin Luther discovered afresh what *grace* means.

Today it seems that we are living in an age in which many truths of the Bible are in eclipse. But on the other hand, we do see something happening that makes all sincere believers glad. What I mean is this: doctrines of the Bible which Christians have not taken seriously enough for a long time are again becoming important to us. We are acquiring a new grasp on them. One of the most relevant, vital issues that we are discovering is the fact that the Church is the Body of Christ. For many years we seemed of the opinion that our churches were all right. But now we are beginning to see our spiritual poverty in the Lord's eyes. And I believe the reason for this poverty is that we, the Church, do not live as the Body of Christ; which consists of many members gifted by the Holy Spirit.

Therefore let us consider three essential thoughts, guided by our text. First, what is the real meaning of the Body of Christ and the relationship of its various parts or members? Secondly, what is the situation among ourselves – that is, do we really live as Christ's Body? Then finally let us ask what are the consequences of such knowledge.

What is the Body of Christ?

First let us try to understand what it means to be the Body of Christ. We all speak about Jesus Christ being the head of the

43

Church. But if someone wants Christ as the head, he must be prepared to become the *body*. As an individual in a congregation, I am not a whole body; I am only a part among other parts. But to these other parts or members I am intrinsically linked – not only on Sunday but throughout every day of the week. Our text says not that we are *like* a body, but that we really *are* a body. The picture of the body is not a parable, but a fact. Therefore, this body actually exists. It is the very nature of the Church. Christ has given His people no other kind of spiritual life than the life in a body which is directly dependent on Christ the Head. All other forms and structures of the Church, even if they seem to be most practicable for the Church, are not fully as they ought to be if the "body" concept is missing. For instance, take the philosophy of church life which sees the Church today *only* as the pastor as a shepherd, and the members as a flock. Such a view of the Church has many good aspects – even some Biblical ones. It is practicable throughout, but there are facets of it that are dangerous. It has at times divided the concept of the body in some congregations. It can bring about a clergy-laity dualism that is quite unbiblical. It puts untold burdens on the pastor-shepherd. If I am a member of the Body of Christ, I must link myself with the other members in all ways of life. We are all parts of the one body – clergy and laity alike. We are all one in Christ. We all share responsibilities. What that means we can see in the following examples:

Let us say somebody is converted and baptized; we should do all we can to help this new Christian, for very often we see new church members fall away after baptism because they fail to get integrated into the full membership of the church. And then the whole body suffers, for we are united one to another. As Paul said, we are members one of another. If I receive God's blessings, the body is blessed as well. It takes part of my blessing. Or if I suffer, the body suffers with me. It shares part of my suffering. If I sin and live in disobedience to the Lord, the whole body will be crippled. The reverse is also true; if the Church is experiencing God's blessing, there will be an effect in my personal life. If there are strained relations in the Church, it stands to reason that I suffer as a member of the strained body. I cannot remain unconcerned if there is a quarrel in the Church. Simply put, we are in this entire enterprise of God together.

The Spirit and the Body

But how can such a love union of people come into existence? The answer is this: the union between Christ the head and His unified yet diversified body takes place through the agency of the Holy Spirit. This is what the Spirit does among God's people. This is His work. Therefore, if anybody desires the fullness of the Spirit, he must be prepared to be a member of Christ's body. You cannot walk with God and refuse to walk with God's people. This is the reason why some Christians are lacking in the full blessing of the Spirit. They are not ready to be a part of or belong to Christ's body. We do not receive the fullness of the Spirit for our personal profit; rather, He is the Gift for functional purposes; namely for service in the body of Christ. And He makes me willing to be a living member of the body.

Thus in the Spirit we get varieties of gifts. In each of us the Spirit is manifested so as to profit the whole Church. It is vitally important that each one acknowledges the individual gifts of every member and also recognizes that he too is the bearer of a gift. Of course, it is legitimate to prove or test members professing to have the gifts. Actually, I would say it is a spiritual duty. But on the other hand, if we have seen that someone indeed possesses a *charisma* of the Spirit, we are bound to accept it as from God.

A Great Need

This is the very point where there is a great need among the churches. Too often the attitude among pastors and elders is that church life functions much better if they do all the work themselves. But we must learn that if anybody despises the *charisma* of a brother or sister, his own gift will inevitably lose spiritual authority. Moreover, to stifle the gifts of others is disastrous to the life of a church. We must realize that the whole church is gifted and that is what makes a church the Body of Christ, rich and glorious and Christ-honouring.

Take two examples. I once knew a man in a church who was gifted to lead the church. Of course such gifted people are very necessary. But this man's personal failure was that he always found faults with those who were preaching. Well, I think sometimes there is something to be said against our preaching, but in this case the man did it because he was basically a fault-finder. Therefore this church leader lost his spiritual authority. The result was that he could not really lead the church in love and mutual respect and thus he became something of a dictator in the church. Finally, the people said, "We will not have your leadership any more," and he lost his place of service.

In another example, there was a sister in the church who had the gift of prophecy. Does that sound strange? In the Bible we find such gifted women. I am well aware of the problems concerning the gift of prophecy. Yet I think we need the *charisma* of prophecy. But because there is a real tendency to error and arrogance, the prophets will have to subject themselves and their prophecies to proper proving by the church. Prophets must therefore be very humble. But back to our sister! Her gift of prophecy seemed to be a genuine *charisma*. But the pastor of this church, and he was a very good, effective preacher, generally spoke against such a gift. Finally, he forbade the sister to speak. But then his sermons began to deteriorate and church members were quite astonished by the poor sermons of this able pastor. Again this illustrates that if somebody does not accept the gifts of God in the brotherhood, he will lose the authority of his own personal *charisma*. The point is, the Church of Jesus is rich because of the *many* gifts. They are numerous and different to meet various needs, and they are distributed to all members of the Church. Everyone has a service to perform for Christ. The varieties of such gifts actually make up the Body of Christ. And it is very clear that in our day – in a changed and still changing world – we need a church membership with the richness of various gifts. Thus co-operation and love must be the nature of the effective church.

How the Body Grows

Now let us learn something about the growing and maturing of the body of Christ. Several years ago I visited a hospital for people with brain injuries. It was a terrible experience. I saw people with faces like old men, but their bodies were like little children. Such illnesses are often caused by an abnormal function of some bodily organ, and it effects the entire development of the body. The same thing can occur in a church. Let me explain what I mean. Let us say, for instance, there is a church where you can hear excellent sermons. There are many brothers who know their Bibles well and know how to interpret the Scriptures. The people in the church are proud of their leaders. They revel in the knowledge of truth. Strangers in the services are deeply impressed by the richness of knowledge in this church. But this is nearly all you can find there. In the same church you will miss other gifts; for example, the gift to evangelize. Despite the church stressing important points on the everyday life of the members, it is not a complete body because there is no one who has the gift of exhortation.

Or take another example. There is a church which has a very good working system of leadership and administration. Churches need that. In this church the members are most generous in their stewardship of money. The church is well known for its social actions. Such churches are respected in our days. But there is a serious lack in the area of spiritual knowledge. They have only a little to say about salvation and reconciliation with God. Well, they speak much about reconciliation but they see it essentially as between man and man – and that is not enough. The Church has more to say. Social action is good, but if it is the only working gift of Christ's body, it resembles the man in the hospital who had an old head but the body of a child. God's will is that we grow up fully. Disproportionate growing is serious, for in the long run it disrupts the entire body.

Our Churches Today

Finally, let us look at the present situation of our churches. The dominating system we have already mentioned is the principle of "shepherd and flock". The pastor is at the top of the church, next to him are several brothers (mostly people of his sympathy) and this group is doing all the work in the church. Now we must admit that the system works reasonably well. Nevertheless, it is a hindrance to the *full* effect of the Holy Spirit. I do not mean to say this system drives away the Spirit, but where a church employs all of its members, that church will be much more blessed and used by the Holy Spirit. It becomes abundantly clear that a church which lives as a body will have the greatest blessings. Of course, it will run the risk of abuse in the use of gifts.

47

You can study the life of the churches at the time of the apostles and you will find problems, but they ran the risk and it was worth it. Thus they were rich in many ways we are not today.

So there we are! The Church is the Body of Christ. And our Lord Jesus Christ is the head. We are His body. And He, our Lord, is inconceivably glorious and rich. Thus as His body on earth we are called to represent His glory and His richness. And this is done by the entire functioning and exercising of the gifts of the Spirit. Therefore, go on to discover your gift; your *charisma.* Go on to be a blessing to all by the exercise of your gift. Thus you shall be a blessing and in turn bless yourself by the many gifts of your brethren and sisters. We are all very rich in the Church. Let's open our treasures and share. And we shall praise the Lord for the glory He will pour out among us. Amen!

Adolf Pohl

The Reverend Adolf Pohl was born on February 3, 1927, in Berlin. He received his theological training at the Hamburg Church Academy (Kirchliche Hochschule in Hamburg) and at the Baptist Theological Seminary in Hamburg. From 1950 to 1957 he served as pastor of one of the East Berlin churches. From 1957 to 1960 he was editor of the Baptist monthly magazine Wort und Werk *of the DDR (East Germany). Since 1959 he has been a teacher and later president of the Baptist Theological Seminary in Buckow (DDR). He is at present teaching New Testament in that institution. He is the author of many books. He was married in 1953 and has four sons.*

Put into practice what you have learned

Adolf Pohl

Philippians 4: 8–9

*Finally, brethren, whatever is true, whatever is
honourable, whatever is just, whatever is pure,
whatever is lovely, whatever is gracious, if there is
any excellence, if there is anything worthy of praise,
think about these things. What you have learned and
received and heard and seen in me, do; and the
God of peace will be with you.*

A command given in the context of the gospel is completely
different from one that is projected, for example, on an army
drill field. Therefore, when the apostle Paul commands, "Put
into practice what you have learned", we hear not only an order
of spiritual authority but one of "permission". What I mean by
the term "permission" is this: you can have the power to put
into actual practice what God commands. And the reason is
clear. God does not present mere theories of love, forgiveness,
renewal, *etc.* His words of promise and command become a
genuine, glowing inner reality. Your sins are truly remitted *here
and now.* His Spirit has actually taken up residence and is in you.
You are now just and pure in His eyes. In Christ, you are strong
and happy. In other words, because of what you have shared in
Christ you now possess the ability to live for Him. Therefore,
work out your own salvation – that is, put it into practice! It is
in this sense that we listen to the biblical admonition for action.

50

The first action to which we have been called is: *Think it over!*
Under certain circumstances, thinking can be a strenuous effort.
This must be true because much is done apparently without any
serious thinking. So many people seemingly leave the thinking
to others and merely follow accepted slogans. They allow themselves to be manipulated by external conditions. They march in
a broad column on a broad way.

The soldiers who crucified Jesus were an example of that.
They did not really know what they were doing, although they
were very involved, with their tormenting of Jesus and their
loud blasphemies. They seemed to do it all as if in a mental fog.
If, twenty years later, they had been brought to trial, accused of
having murdered the guiltless Jew, they probably would have
cried very angrily, "We? Do you want us to take responsibility
for the death of this man when all of the people were shouting
'Crucify him!' Did not all of the officials support his death,
even the theologians? We were in the pressure and the emotion
of that moment." Under such circumstances thinking can often
avert tragedy; and the absence of it can be disastrous.

Our text calls for the kind of thinking that results in positive
action. The eight things enumerated in Paul's writing, the eight
things we are to think about, are eight strokes with which he
outlines a beautiful picture. It is the picture of the spiritually
healthy man, one who is mature in every aspect of life. It is a
portrait of a really human person; the kind of person God wants
us to be and what our own conscience demands that we be.

In contrast to that picture, Paul in another place describes
the disordered man. He told young Timothy: "You must face
the fact: the final age of this world is to be a time of troubles.
Men will love nothing but money and self; they will be arrogant,
boastful, and abusive; with no respect for parents, no gratitude,
no piety, no natural affection; they will be implacable in their
hatreds, scandalmongers, intemperate and fierce, strangers to all
goodness, traitors, adventurers, swollen with self importance"
(2 Tim. 3: 1–4). Obviously, this kind of man with his selfish
lifestyle presses in on us from every side.

And we must face it, this man has an influence upon us; we are
all at times tempted by him. The possibility exists that he may
even pull us down to his level of life. Therefore, Paul in essence

urges: "Dear brothers, be diligent, do not let the picture of the healthy, godly man disappear or be distorted. Be absolutely true and noble towards everybody and everything. Keep justice although injustice is spreading; relate in love and compassion to all men although love is growing cold among people; be pure in an unchaste neighbourhood." Simply put; *"Be Christlike in character and thought."*

The Glory of Forgiveness

We can clearly see what this is all about. It is about the creation of the new man amidst a decaying world. True, at one time we all belonged to those who "did not know what they were doing". But then we heard Jesus' prayer from the cross: "Father, forgive them; they do not know what they are doing." Suddenly we discovered that there is forgiveness and we need not go on our foolish way until the bitter end.

And how radically forgiveness changes a man! Forgiveness brings cleansing from every kind of wrong. Forgiveness gives a man a new spirit and inspires both the will and the deed for God's own chosen purpose. Forgiveness brings salvation to body and soul. Forgiveness "normalizes" life. Mark's gospel tells of a totally disordered man who accepted the kingdom of God. After his meeting with the Lord Jesus Christ his old friends came and were astonished to see him "sitting there clothed and in his right mind" (Mark 5: 15).

The wonder of the saved man comes, as we can see, from the wonder of forgiveness. He who has been forgiven much is able to love much. And he who is loving is able to think clearly and distinctly. Much love and clear and distinct thinking is the basis for everything good and meaningful in life. But thinking alone is not enough. We then have to get very practical and take:

The Second Step

Put it into practice! Paul reminds the Christians in Philippi of their experience which speaks of a very basic Christian principle. He states, "What you have received and learned and seen and heard . . . " This is to imply that not only did they hear thrilling sermons and great teaching that fascinated them, there was also a deep spiritual desire for learning among the hearers. And it was not learning in a merely formal, academic sense. They sought for *practical* learning. Again, it was not an understanding of unreal mystical depths they were after. The understanding they desired could be "seen and tasted".

Those times were unforgettable hours, when spiritual milk and honey were flowing. We have all had such hours in our spiritual pilgrimage with Christ. But this stream of truth and power is always intended to be channelled into a life of practical Christian service and power. Very deliberately Paul said, ". . . put it into practice! " The stream of church life is never meant to be like a waterfall falling down from the cliffs where people can come from everywhere to say admiringly: "How beautiful! " Being "beautiful" is not the aim of the Church. The word of God having been communicated and believed has to be *put into practice.* When did we last say to our Lord, "Dear Jesus, I have no courage and no special abilities, but trusting in your word, I will do what you want me to do. I will practice what your Spirit lays on my heart." These actions are not necessarily based on our education, abilities or traditions, but on the word and power of Jesus Christ. Therefore, we can do all things, under the Spirit's leadership and guidance.

A Life of Conflict Is Certain

You ask, will not such action lead to conflicts? Of course! Life under absolute obedience to Jesus Christ is dangerous. Certainly it is costly. But at the same time, putting into practice the commands of Christ is our only hope of preservation. John writes: "Because you have kept my command, I will also keep you." And Paul also makes the point concerning the wonderful preservation of God by adding: ". . . and the God of peace will be with you."

Let me illustrate this principle with a comparison. In the daylight we can go up the stairs without any help, but in the darkness we need banisters. Jesus' commandments are the banister for us in the night. And this banister alone can keep us safe in the difficult and dangerous life we live every day. Therefore Christ commands: "Take hold of the banister. Put into practice what you have learned, regardless of the cost. Do not compromise, no matter how hard someone is pressuring you." And it is in putting into practice these commands of our Lord Jesus that we find our only preservation. That is why the psalmist prayed; "The wicked have waited for me to destroy me: but I will consider thy testimonies. My soul is continually in my hand yet do I not forget thy love. Thy testimonies have I taken as an heritage forever: for they are the rejoicing of my heart."

Our Task

The Church of Jesus Christ has the task to speak about everything she has learned from Jesus and to put it into practice. There is no other reason for the existence of the Church. Giving up this basis, the Church becomes superfluous. If such a case ever develops, the time of her preservation is over – and should be.

What marvellous grace God has shown us in His Son, Jesus Christ! What love He has proved in that He has erected this "banister" and has put our hand on it so that we are allowed to stay quite close to Him. May we always fulfill His expectation for us and accomplish our task.   Amen!

Fritz Petersen

The Reverend Fritz Petersen was born on September 12, 1926, at Loquard near Emden. He studied at Wiedenest from 1946 to 1948 and from 1948 to 1950 in Hamburg. His service as a Baptist pastor has been: 1950 to 1960 Rostock, 1960 to 1969 Luckenwalde. Since 1969 he has served as pastor of a Baptist church in Leipzig.

The Good Shepherd

Fritz Petersen

John 10: 11–16

*I am the good shepherd. The good shepherd lays
down his life for the sheep. He who is a hireling
and not a shepherd, whose own the sheep are not,
sees the wolf coming and leaves the sheep and flees;
and the wolf snatches them and scatters them. He
flees because he is a hireling and cares nothing for
the sheep. I am the good shepherd; I know my own
and my own know me, as the Father knows me
and I know the Father; and I lay down my life for
the sheep. And I have other sheep, that are not
of this fold; I must bring them also, and they will
heed my voice. So there shall be one flock, one
shepherd.*

We all know how easy it is to form an opinion of someone
although we may have never personally seen the individual. From
some story or some chance remark about him, we often picture
him with distinct features, personality, character, *etc.* But when
we get to know him in person, or are shown his photograph, we
usually discover that our preconceived image does not prove
correct at all and has little relation to reality. We usually find
we imagined him a quite different individual; and we may be
disappointed or else rather pleasantly surprised.

Such is often the case when we think of Jesus as "the Good
Shepherd". Probably no other pictorial representation of Jesus is
so popular and so well known, yet at the same time so easily
mistaken. We normally conceive the thought of a shepherd as
someone meek, tender, or even somewhat too soft. Moreover,
the shepherd idea usually presents to our imagination the picture

of a shepherd boy or an old man. For example, at the Christmas season in the nativity dramas the children who play the shepherds' roles attempt to screw up their faces and to disguise their voices. They wear old, worn out bath robes and carry pastoral staves, and these staves are hardly for chasing away a wild beast with vigour and life. Rather, they are for leaning upon as old, tired men. Thus our picture of the shepherd – at least unconsciously – has been coloured by just such representations.

An Error to Avoid

The tragedy is the association we may make with Jesus when we call Him "the Good Shepherd". If our image of a shepherd is perverted, it is all too easy to push Him aside as an untimely idea, irrelevant for our lives, and say He has nothing for our day and time. The children at Sunday school may well sing: "Jesus Friend of little children be a Friend to me!" But the adult may well miss the whole idea. What is the *true* Shepherd of the gospel? What is the genuine biblical figure of Jesus as the Shepherd of all men's souls? First of all, it must be made clear that the shepherd of the Bible has little in common with the contemporary shepherd in modern civilized countries who pastures his sheep. The work of a shepherd in past cultures was hard; he had to take many risks, his work was dangerous and responsible. For example, when David was to take up the fight against Goliath he reported to King Saul from his own experiences: "Thy servant kept his father's sheep, and there came a lion, and a bear, and took a lamb out of the flock. I went out after him, and smote him, and delivered it out of his mouth; and when he arose against me, I caught him by his beard and smote him, and slew him. Thy servant slew both the lion and the bear" (1 Samuel 17: 34–36).

In biblical culture, it was normal for the owner himself or his sons to pasture the herd. The professional shepherd took meticulous care of the sheep, with deep concern and full devotion for his task. The sheep were his sole fortune; the entire resource of the family. Therefore, the shepherd summoned all his strength to defend the flock, risking his life for his sheep under constant danger from thieves or wild beasts. At times, however, circumstances might dictate that one had to entrust a hired man or servant with the flock. There was always the probability that such a man would not risk his life for the sheep; he might well flee at the moment of impending danger. He priced his own life higher than that of the animals entrusted to him. It is in this setting that Jesus made a very clear distinction between himself and a hireling, saying: "I am the good shepherd. The good shepherd lays down his life for his sheep. But he who is a hireling and not a shepherd, whose own the sheep are not, sees the wolf coming, and leaves the sheep and flees; and the wolf snatches them and scatters them" (John 10: 11–12).

Jesus the True Shepherd

Now this parable obviously presents Jesus as the "good shepherd". But we must see the idea of the shepherd through first century eyes if we are to get the impact of the imagery. There is nothing soft and weak here. On the contrary, we find ourselves confronted with a manly fighter who battles for His flock. Five times in this shepherd passage in John chapter 10 the Lord speaks of giving His life for the sheep.

Jesus thus gives a profound and unique interpretation to His death; His way to the cross is to be a fight with "the wolf", with Satan. Men are constantly threatened by this dread enemy and Jesus does not want to leave them at the mercy of that wicked foe. He is prepared to retrieve them from the enemy even if, in the end, He should die for His sheep. He has taken up the fight with "the wolf" in true loyalty to His work as the shepherd – even though it cost Him His life. But is this wolf stronger than our Lord? Has Jesus fallen a mere victim to the enemy? No, and again I say No! That would be to misunderstand the facts totally if we would interpret the death of Jesus in that fashion. Our Lord made it quite clear that He has power to lay His life down: "No man takes it from me" (John 10, 18). His death meant that *He* laid down His life willingly and purposely for His sheep. This is made clear by His statement on the night He was taken prisoner: "If therefore you seek me, let these go their way" (John 18: 8). Thus He stands as a true shepherd, defending His disciples, protecting them and ultimately saving them by His death. He went to death of His own accord with a view to safeguarding them and to preserve them from the onslaughts of the enemy.

Jesus the Great Shepherd

And such support and protection did not end with Jesus' death. It is wonderfully true that the good shepherd gave His life for His sheep (John 10: 11), but at the same moment we hear: "Death could not hold him." In the epistle to the Hebrews we read: "God brought again from the dead our Lord Jesus, the great shepherd of the sheep" (13: 20). The crucified Jesus is risen. Thus He is not only the good shepherd, but the "great shepherd". All power is given unto Him in heaven and in earth (Matthew 28: 20). He stands as the powerful resurrected Christ, and as the great Shepherd supports us to the utmost. In Him we have a Shepherd *and a Lord.* He is one who protects His people and delivers them from *all* evil, even if the enemy seems powerful and mighty. Jesus Himself said, "They shall never perish, neither shall any man pluck them out of my hand" (John 10: 28). And behind Him is the Father, and no man is able to pluck them out of His Father's hand. What a consolation lies in the fact that we have such a Shepherd!

One of the most intriguing places to see when one visits Rome is the catacombs. These ancient underground passages with their sepulchre vaults are where the first Christians had their meetings. On the surface above they were being hunted and taken prisoner and often thrown to the wild beasts. Below the surface in the catacombs, however, they could secretly congregate in safety. It was also there that the Christians buried their own dead. Sometimes the bones alone were the only remains of a martyr who had given his life for the testimony of Christ. Often engraved on these tombs were pictures of Christ. It is interesting that these old Christian pictorial representations often show Jesus as the good shepherd; the shepherd with the staff in His hand and a lamp in His arms! It was that very picture which was meant to comfort the first Christian Martyr-Church. To them there was nothing weak and soft in such a concept. On the contrary, to them Jesus was the good shepherd who was equal to His task. They had perfect confidence in Him to deliver His people – if need be even through death into the other world.

The Relevancy of the Concept

Now surely it is true that, regardless of our present circumstances, we all need such a shepherd who supports our cause in that strong way. And the word of the good shepherd has a most relevant meaning in our day, for the "wolf" can clearly be heard again. At least he can be heard howling from afar. There are countries where the Christians are no longer permitted to come together freely to worship and to hear a sermon. Thank God, we still have that opportunity. But in any case, being a Christian means to stand decidedly on the side of Christ regardless of the cost. That may mean we have to make sacrifices in our professional life. Standing for Christ may very well hinder a man's means for getting gain. And who can say what is in store for us in the future in the way of persecution? The future only God knows, but the times of the wolves are always times for the good shepherd to show His power. It is in just such a time of danger that we believers can be sure of the care Jesus offers, and we can feel safe in Him; and this is also true for the small as well as the large concerns of our daily life. We have a shepherd who is personally and deeply interested in us. Calvary is the proof of His love. And He who gave His life for the sheep is the same "yesterday, today, and forever". As the psalmist said: "Lord, thou hast been our dwelling place in all generations" (Ps. 90: 1).

Again, Jesus speaks of the good shepherd in still another sense. He said, "I am the good shepherd" and "I know my sheep and am known of mine, as the Father knoweth me even so know I the Father" (John 10: 14–15). This verse can be best understood in the context of the shepherd life of Jesus' times. The shepherd was in close relation to his sheep. He was in constant contact with them. Even during the night he was near his flock, as we can clearly see from the Nativity report. Therefore, the shepherd knew all his sheep; he even knew them by name (John 10: 14).

This, of course, is cause for cheer. This truth should fill us with joy. In our age man is constantly being thrust into a nameless crowd; we are being numbered and classified continually. "What is the worth of the individual human being?" We often are tempted to ask this basic question. But Jesus knows our names. He knows what we individually are and what are our deepest personal needs. This is how he knew Nathanael; "Before that Philip called thee, when thou was under the fig tree, I saw thee" (John 1: 48). He also had deep insight into the experience and personhood of the Samaritan woman; "Thou hast had five

60

husbands and he whom thou now hast is not thy husband" (John 4: 18). But he did not despise her for that reason. He understood her so that He might be able to help her. "I know them!" "I know *you*!" That is an assurance which gives true joy and meaning to life. It is in accordance with this "I know you" that He takes care of us. His knowing us influences His actions towards us. In a word, He meets us on the basis of our personal needs.

Look how closely the shepherd lives among his sheep, how he deals with the animals quite individually as their needs require. Here he ruffles one animal's coat, there he strokes another tenderly. With another sheep he looks to see whether the bruised leg has healed or whether it must get another treatment with oil. Another time he takes a pebble, throwing it after a sheep which has moved away too far from the flock to drive it back into the fold. In another case he will send the shepherd dog to chase the sheep back, or even "bite it back" into the flock.

Can we not in the same way see our Saviour Shepherd in His dealings with us? How often does He influence the course of our life? Sometimes He is bound to throw a pebble or a stone, or must even send the shepherd dog – some affliction – lest we come to some calamity. It is so easy to move away from Him and His flock, and even though He allows hardships to come into our life, He is most kindly disposed toward us. He knows what we need.

To what extent the care of the true shepherd extends can be seen from His words: "I give them eternal life" (verse 28). Now it must be made clear that this is no promise of a rich, easy, luxurious pasture with respect to our earthly conditions. It is easy for us to think that in the fellowship of Christ everything disagreeable should be eliminated and that the Christian should walk only on sunny hills. Jesus has not promised that everything will go smoothly in our life. But it is a meaningful life. It is a life of final victory. It has purpose. His gift to us is *everlasting life*. He says, "I am come that they might have life and that they might have it more abundantly" (verse 10). Though affliction may come, still life in Christ is the *abundant* life.

But be assured of this; whatever you expect of life, whatever deserves the name of "life" in any ultimate sense, will be found *in Jesus Christ alone*. Satisfaction of the inmost needs, sins forgiven, a right relationship with God and others; these things only Jesus can give to those who believe on Him. And this eternal life begins in the here and now, fed from the source of the "upper world", that is, fellowship with Jesus. And when we are made perfect, at the resurrection, we shall attain it in its fullness. When we have reached that determined mark and are united forever with our Lord and with the believers of all times, then that word of the Lord will be fulfilled when He said, "and there shall be one fold and one shepherd" (verse 16).

The Necessary Prerequisite

Now all these wonderful truths apply to ourselves, provided we belong to the flock of Christ. Can Jesus count us in his fold? That is the issue. In His analogy of Himself as the good shepherd He draws a sharp dividing line between Himself and the hireling. Likewise, He also draws a dividing line between those who are His sheep and the others of whom He must say: "You believe not because you are not of my sheep" (verse 26). On the one side are the believers, on the other side are those who persist in unbelief. This dividing line which separates men from one another can be seen throughout the entire Bible. Cain and Abel, sons of the same parents, were so different before God that He accepted the offering of one and had no respect to the offering of the other. There were two malefactors hanging on two other crosses beside Jesus; one of them went into paradise with Him, the other to his own place. At the day of Pentecost a number were filled with the Holy Spirit whereas others were mocking: "These men are full of new wine." Such a partition wall divides all mankind even today; invisible indeed, yet still very real. Such a wall may even go through a family or even through a congregation at church.

Moreover, this is the only dividing line acknowledged by the Lord of Heaven. There are many dividers which separate peoples and nations from one another. Man draws lines between colours of the skin or between adherents of different creeds, or barriers between different political views or between people of different social standing, etc. All these boundary lines are irrelevant in the eyes of God. Before God there are only those who hear the voice of the good shepherd and follow Him, and those who are deaf to His voice and turn away from Him.

Therefore, we must face the question as to where we belong; whether we are sheep of the good shepherd, or whether Jesus must say to us, "You are not of my sheep."

Our Lord makes it quite clear how His sheep can be recognized: "My sheep hear my voice." They have an open ear for the care-taking, shepherd-voice. They take their place in the "flock" wherever the truth of God is preached. They hunger and thirst for the word of God. So they read it daily, they occupy themselves with it and are concerned with it. They love Jesus and His word and open their heart to Him.

This "being open" to the voice of the good shepherd is naturally coupled with being deaf to other voices. At the beginning of His parable Jesus put it like this: "When the shepherd putteth forth his own sheep, he goes before them; for they know his voice and the sheep follow him. And a stranger they will not follow but will flee from him, for they know not the voice of strangers" (verse 4 and 5). In case a stranger comes, even though he may be clad in the coat of a true shepherd and uses a voice similar to the one of the true shepherd, the sheep will take no notice. They go on pasturing and will not be disturbed. The strange voice of the false shepherd cannot move them. Likewise, the disciples of Jesus are not deceived. They do not allow themselves to be taken in by the many voices clamouring for attention. Yes, they are subjected to many voices, many impressions, many temptations. But at the same time, they know that they must not listen to all that is presented or suggested to them. They must learn to "switch off". Above all, they learn to judge what does not coincide with the voice of Jesus, and what must therefore be refused.

Naturally, it is particularly dangerous to the flock of Jesus Christ if the voice of the stranger comes with pious words. And it is true that false prophets *often* come in sheep's clothing, but inwardly they are ravening wolves. Here it is imperative to be on the alert and to listen to Jesus' words most intently in order to distinguish His voice from that of a false prophet.

Further, "My sheep hear my voice and they follow me." That is the second feature of His sheep. Those who belong to Him and listen to the voice of the shepherd follow Him in obedience and

63

Christian fellowship. It is from that basic attitude of surrender to Jesus Christ that decisions are made and the course of action is chosen. The word of the gospel becomes a living fact and decides one's lifestyle. Sometimes you may hear a Christian say: "Indeed, that is in the Bible, but you can't be so insistent about it. Where would we be if we should adapt our lives to all the biblical regulations?" But a Christian in genuine fellowship with Christ cannot speak like that. It is an essential feature of the sheep of Christ that they not only know the voice of the shepherd, they also *follow* that voice.

The Seeking Shepherd

Do we recognize that attitude of rebellion in ourselves at times? I am afraid that applies to a good many. Perhaps someone will say, "In former times it was well with me. I loved the Lord and His word above all. But I must admit that I strayed away rather far from Him in the course of time." Or another one may state, "It has struck me that I do not yet truly belong to the flock of Jesus. Up to now I have always evaded a decision." To those we may candidly say: "Indeed, there are lost sheep, erring and straying sheep. You may be one of these, but there is also a good Shepherd who longingly seeks you. He is the seeking Shepherd who goes after the lost sheep until He finds it. He willingly leaves the ninety-nine to seek the one lost sheep. He walks through thorny bushes, over wild, rocky ground for the sake of that one. This is His saving, seeking, caring love. Don't you feel Him seeking you? Don't you now hear Him calling you? He longs to help you, to bring you back to His fold. He is the true Shepherd. He well merits our confidence, trust, love, and obedience. Amen!

Wolfgang Klempert

The Reverend Wolfgang Klempert was born on February 4, 1931, in Gorlitz. After finishing school with honours, he spent a four-year apprenticeship in the trade of an organ builder. Then, hearing the divine call to the ministry, he spent 1954 to 1958 in the Theological Seminary in Hamburg. He has served the following churches as pastor: 1958 to 1962 – Jessen; 1962 to 1968 – Jessen and Lutherstadt Wittenberg. Since 1968 he has been pastor in Magdeburg and Burg. He is the leader of the local Association of Churches.

The victory God gives

Wolfgang Klempert

Exodus 14: 8–22, 30–31

*And the Lord hardened the heart of Pharaoh king
of Egypt and he pursued the people of Israel as they
went forth defiantly. The Egyptians pursued them,
all Pharaoh's horses and chariots and his horsemen
and his army, and overtook them encamped at the
sea, by Pihahiroth, in front of Baalzephon.*

*When Pharaoh drew near, the people of Israel
lifted up their eyes, and behold, the Egyptians were
marching after them; and they were in great fear.
And the people of Israel cried out to the Lord;
and they said to Moses, "Is it because there are
no graves in Egypt that you have taken us away to
die in the wilderness? What have you done to us,
in bringing us out of Egypt? Is not this what we
said to you in Egypt, 'Let us alone and let us serve
the Egyptians'? For it would have been better for us to
serve the Egyptians than to die in the wilderness."*

*And Moses said to the people, "Fear not, stand
firm, and see the salvation of the Lord, which he will
work for you today; for the Egyptians whom you
see today, you shall never see again. The Lord will
fight for you, and you have only to be still." The
Lord said to Moses, "Why do you cry to me? Tell
the people of Israel to go forward. Lift up your
rod, and stretch out your hand over the sea and
divide it, that the people of Israel may go on dry
ground through the sea. And I will harden the
hearts of the Egyptians, so that they shall go in
after them and I will get glory over Pharaoh and
all his host, his chariots, and his horsemen. And the
Egyptians shall know that I am the Lord, when I*

have gotten glory over Pharaoh, his chariots and his
horsemen."

Then the angel of God who went before the host
of Israel moved and went behind them; and the
pillar of cloud moved from before them and stood
behind them, coming between the host of Egypt
and the host of Israel. And there was the cloud and
the darkness; and the night passed without one
coming near the other all night.

Then Moses stretched out his hand over the sea;
and the Lord drove the sea back by a strong east
wind all night, and made the sea dry land, and the
waters were divided. And the people of Israel went
into the midst of the sea on dry ground, the waters
being a wall to them on their right hand and on
their left.

Thus the Lord saved Israel that day from the
hand of the Egyptians; and Israel saw the Egyptians
dead upon the seashore. And Israel saw the great
work which the Lord did against the Egyptians, and
the people feared the Lord; and they believed in
the Lord and his servant Moses.

This passage is an instructional word, a personal lesson from
God on the secret of His miracles – and on the secret of our
belief and unbelief. If the reader will seriously attempt to grasp
the lesson, noticing the divine suggestion contained in these
verses, he will profit greatly from it.

The situation of Israel as they stood facing the Red Sea with
the Egyptian army behind them has at all times been a classical
example of desperation. It is a perfect expression of coming to
the absolute end of one's own resources. There is no one who
can say that the hopelessness of his case is greater than was that
of the Israelites.

The Perfect Dilemma

Imagine those people! They were for all practical purposes in
the clutches of the overwhelming power of Egypt; that highly

trained military power which was ready to roll over the fleeing slaves. They saw Israel as wretched ants, a defenceless, unprotected mob. In front of God's people was the sea, behind them the enemy; no hope, all seemed lost. The followers of Moses began to imagine that the exodus was not God's work at all, that they had been brought out of the land of Egypt so they would all perish.

So often we feel life is a perplexing dilemma. Often our situation is much like that of the children of Israel. We seem to be in a jam between the sea and the enemy with no way out; complete despair overtakes us.

At such a time there is only one question; with the sea on one side and the enemy behind we are forced to ask, "Where is God?" This question will be still more urgent if we grasp what precipitated the situation. The incredible thing of that story is, this was no blind accident – God himself had manoeuvered his people into this seemingly hopeless situation.

After the children of Israel made their exodus out of Egypt, they set out in an easterly direction with a view to going to Canaan to the north. But God led them to the south-east, barring their way to the north. This thrust them towards the sea, to the bitter lakes in the south near the region of the present day Suez Canal. Then God hardened the heart of Pharaoh and the Egyptian monarch repented that he had let the people go. The heart of that tyrant rose to a boiling rage. He eagerly got his host of horsemen and chariots together. Quickly they mobilized for the definite purpose of annihilating Israel. But could God steer His people into such a desperate situation? It seems incredible. Are they to come to an end? Yet, He is the Lord and must be followed at any cost.

Is There an Answer?

With an appalling and fathomless calmness – God's own calmness – the Lord said to Moses in this hopeless dilemma, "I will show the salvation of the Lord today, I will be honoured before Pharaoh that the Egyptians may know that I am the Lord." The children of Israel saw the sea before them, the enemy behind them. Is there a way out? What are they to do now? What do pious people do in such a situation?

As usual, the Bible in this passage is strictly realistic. There is no report of heroes of faith or of a grand, pious attitude. We read the bare truth: they were sore afraid and cried unto the Lord. Moreover, they reproached Moses; "Why hast thou taken us away to die in the wilderness? It would have been better to serve the Egyptians." No heroes; the people murmur. This is the attitude of the "pious people of God" to their difficult situation. They cry because they have the sea before them and the enemy behind. And murmuring against God, they complain, "Better to serve the Egyptians than to die in the wilderness. Were there no graves in Egypt that thou hast taken us away?" Death is bound to overpower us, they thought. It would be better to have at least some security, some kind of life rather than dying. How futile! To die in a nameless situation is utterly meaningless. Oh, that we had not left!

This is the very essence of what happens to us emotionally when the waters of adversity rise and threaten to drown us. When refugees are shot at by pilots in their war planes; when the children freeze in the snowstorm and are left on the side of the road; when everything collapses in on us; then there is only one way out we think – *capitulation.* Or, could there be another possibility – *miracles?* But can miracles actually happen? Is there a God who works miracles? Can He do what nobody would have thought possible? Does He actually perform miracles? The anwer is emphatically: YES. He is alive and does wonders. How foolish to say "God is dead." "He that sitteth in heaven shall laugh. The Lord shall have them in derision" (Ps. 2: 4). He lives, and is a miracle-working God.

One Man is Enough

But it takes faith to see God at work. Yet, if only one single person is open-minded to the dealings of God, the situation is not hopeless. The tragedy of Israel's situation is that the whole people are in desperation and seemingly faithless. They cry; they are afraid; they murmur and quarrel. But thank God there is one person to whom God can address His word. He says to Moses, the man of faith, "Tell the people of Israel to go." Now look at what Moses told them. He said they were to go on straight ahead – into the sea. That would be suicide, impossible, the faithless multitude thought. Indeed, it would be suicide without the direct leadership of God. But faith believes in miracles. To reckon with a miracle in that destitute situation means to believe in a miracle-working God. But by faith it is not a hazardous action; rather, it is obedience to the word of God. And obedience of that kind always leads to life and victory.

This is the word which brightens every letter of this old story; the report of the man who does not merely rationalize. Man looks on the outward appearance. Faith reckons with that which is above him, and that means believing.

Moses then, in faith, gives a word of command: "Fear ye not, stand still, and see the salvation of the Lord." In other words, "Don't be afraid, either of the sea or of the enemy." The reason? The Lord is fighting for you. That changes everything, and that means believing the naked word, the mere guarantee of God, to stand still and see *the salvation of the Lord*. He has brought you from Egypt, not to allow you to be drowned like rats in the sea, but to show you who is Lord of all the earth. *The Lord will fight for you and you shall hold your peace.* You are to keep quiet. Stop your murmuring, keep your peace, leave your fears, let go and listen and see what God is able to do.

What we are able to do, we know. We know the limits of the human. But *believing* means to reckon with what God is capable of doing.

> Onward Christian soldiers . . .
> We go at our Master's command
> And our Lord is with us.

Forward! Directly into the sea! That is the command of God.

But can God expect his people to believe, especially in such a situation? He is directing them towards the sea. Certainly God cannot demand that! Yet going straight ahead in the direction of the sea, that's what it means to believe.

The Answer Is Coming

But the answer is coming. It takes merely a gesture, a movement of the hand: "Lift up your rod." And God makes a way within the sea. He provides the way out where no human being can see a solution.

Thus, if you writhe under strain and disbelief like a fish on

70

dry land; if you have come to the end of hope – then God can show you His salvation. It is in the moments of greatest darkness that He brings His people through the water.

This is the miracle God accomplished for Israel. Night falls, the enemy is hindered, they become disoriented. God comes in between His people and the Egyptians. And "a strong east wind made the sea go back and made the sea dry land and the children of Israel went into the midst of the sea upon dry ground." And the Egyptians followed only to be destroyed. When the morning rose the shore was covered with the dead of the Egyptians. What a victory!

Oh, true, it is an incredible story and you may accept or refuse the idea that God works miracles. But God does the "impossible". We are only to believe. May it be our prayer: "Oh, Lord, open our eyes to see the truth and reality of this great old story." And God can bring His enlightenment through the greatest darkness. That's a wonderful truth; and how desperately we need to believe God. He can cause the waters to retreat and provide a way through any sea. He knows a way out where no one can find a solution.

Three issues seize our attention right here:

First, Israel's situation by the sea shore being encircled by the enemy is very similar to our situation in Eastern Germany. We should have no illusion with regard to present day realities. We are no longer in that era called "Christendom". Rather, we are in an epoch of adversity against the Church. We can no longer, therefore, rest in a moral piousness as in the times of a comfortable yesterday. We must see life as a courageous venture with God. That is the situation with the Church of God – and our personal situation as well. It is true for all, let us have no illusions. In front of us is the "sea"; tomorrow, the future, the darkness, things which you do not know and which you do not hold in your hands. And behind us is the "enemy"; yesterday the past, life with its burden and trespasses, which are expressed in our faces and which we cannot simply shake off. And between the future and the past we stand in the midst with fear and trembling.

This is often the situation in our families, in our professions, in many aspects of life. We do not, of course, often admit it. We find it so easy to hide behind the noise and the pace of daily events. But when we get desperate and hopeless in our anxieties

71

and are forced to face reality, then we ask, "Why did that happen to me and why does God pressure me like that? Am I, or is our generation, any worse than the ones before us; and do we not need some security?" We are just like the Israelite people at the sea, murmuring and complaining. The scriptures call such situations "temptations" or "testings". What does God say at such a time? What is His response to our questioning? God's answer is: "The Lord will fight for you and you will keep your peace." Oh, if we could only learn that!

The next point is: God is mightily at work in all of this. "Stand still and see the salvation of the Lord," Moses said. God cannot only cleave the sea for His people that they may walk through it; the Son of God Himself walked through the sea of testing and anxiety when He faced death to prepare the way for us. Now we can never say, "Here is a difficulty where God has no answer." Jesus Christ has purchased a way for all to have peace and eternal life. Jesus has tasted death for all mankind. He is the pioneer of every aspect of our faith.

Actually, the story of the passage through the Red Sea is a foreshadowing of the great mystery of redemption from the powers of the darkness. God Himself, in His Son Jesus Christ, has passed through this sea to be the victor over the powers of the deep. Jesus has made Himself one with us so as to make our footsteps sure through the forgiveness and mercy of God. The secret of the victory of God is revealed in Calvary when Jesus made the way for you and me. He can make a new man out of a poor fellow, change him into His beloved child, giving the security of forgiveness, of a new life, and eternal salvation.

The glad tidings of the old story therefore is: there is victory in all the circumstances of life. God works miracles. The way forward is open. Jesus leads the way. Therefore, follow Him!

Thirdly, where does the miracle end? Where does it have its final outcome? In your own heart, if you are believing.

This old story thus turns into an unmistakable call to believe in the midst of all situations, even when one it tempted to complain, murmur, and bring accusations against God. Therefore, listen to the personal appeal: You are called by Jesus Christ to believe in the same way as these people; even in the seemingly hopeless situation and in the dark night of the soul. The call is: "Tell the children of Israel they shall go forward." In the name of our Lord and Saviour Jesus Christ we encourage each other. You shall go forward, take courage and be of good cheer. Move forward into the darkness of the future. You may rely upon the presence of God, humbly but quite confidently. You may go forward, even in the direction of your own personal "sea".

What kind of a sea is that? It is the same water over which our Lord walked in the fourth watch of the night. The same water on which Peter walked, and when he began to sink, Jesus stretched forth His hand and caught him. The same water of which we read in John 21 that Jesus stood on the shore when the morning was come; and the same sea of which the Bible tells us, "And there was no more sea" (Rev. 21:1). Therefore, *fear not;* that is, believing, put fear aside; that is your spiritual exercise every morning.

Fear originates when we reckon only with ourselves or with human strength, when we feel pressed in both in front and behind. But fear not! Between you and any darkness is Jesus. Believe! *Stand still and see the salvation of the Lord.* That has nothing to do with unreal enthusiasm. You trust God's word – and His word is always truth. And in this truth the power of miracle is realized. "God can!"

So there is assurance: *The Lord will fight for you and you will keep your peace.* That means dying to one's self. We must cut loose from the human things of our life and be like beggars. We must learn to keep our peace before God: "In returning and rest shall ye be saved. In quietness and confidence shall be your strength" (Isa. 30:15).

But being a real people of God is not bitter silence. On the contrary, it is a *trustful* silence, leaving everything to God, without interfering. That means listening to the voice of the Holy Spirit who asks you to risk it all with God. It means placing into the hands of God your own very heart and life. That is believing, that is faith in God.

And you will see the salvation of the Lord. Of course, it may not all quite coincide with what you imagined, but you will know salvation has come.

Thus this story has its climax in the personal decision of faith. This story has its end, and should end, in the victory of God in your life as you give yourself to Him through faith in Jesus Christ. Will you do it now? Amen.

Sermons from
ROMANIA

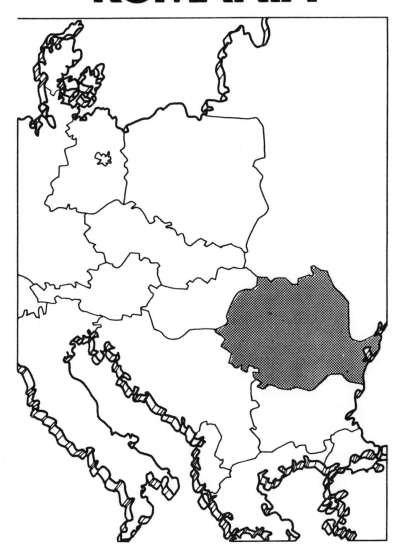

Petru Popovici

*The Reverend Petru Popovici was born in Harrisburg,
Pennsylvania, USA, on September 12, 1918, His parents
were immigrants from Romania, where they returned in
1921 with their children.* In 1932 he heard the voice of
Jesus and surrendered his life to Christ. He studied in
the Baptist Theological Seminary of Romania between
1937 and 1940.

*In 1945 he was chosen pastor of the First Baptist
Church in Arad, Romania where he worked for eight
years. In 1953 he accepted the pastorate of the First
Baptist Church in Timisoara, Romania. The following
two sermons were preached in that church.*

He translated into Romanian The Bible for Today's
World *and* Did Man Just Happen? *by W. A. Criswell,*
All of Grace *by C. H. Spurgeon, and* The Country I
Love Best *by Oswald Smith. Also he is the author of*
Is the Bible True? *and* Children of the Bible.

*Now he lives in Bell, California and is pastor of the
Romanian Baptist Church of the Los Angeles area.
With his brother Dr Alexa Popovici, he shares a daily
gospel radio programme to Romania through HCJB.*

The weaknesses of man and the power of the almighty God

Petru Popovici

Daniel 2: 10, 28

There is not a man upon the earth that can . . .
But there is a God in heaven . . .

How I pray that the Holy Spirit would lay upon your hearts the sacred word of God in such a fashion that it could never be forgotten. Like a man who finds a precious gem of great value and seeks to preserve it and keep it in a safe and secret place, so must we keep the word of God hidden in our heart, soul, and mind; for it is more precious than the most valuable gem that man could ever discover.

Some may think that these verses from Daniel are not particularly important. Nevertheless, consider them! For tomorrow they may prove to be very useful and vitally necessary in the walk of your Christian life. Thus I pray that God will pour out His blessings upon the Word for every Christian – and non-Christian as well.

The King's Dream

The text that I want to speak on is found in Daniel, chapter 2. The chapter opens with a picture of Babylon in the year 603 BC during the second year of King Nebuchadnezzar's reign. It was an era of peace and the king was at leisure in his palace. But then King Nebuchadnezzar was taken with a dream that greatly

78

puzzled and disturbed him.

Now Solomon says that some dreams find their content in present day problems, while others are of past events. But there are also dreams that foretell the future and point to what tomorrow has in store. An example of this phenomenon that perhaps you yourselves have experienced is to dream of someone whom you do not even know, and then the next day to bump into him on the street or meet him by coincidence. But there can be other dreams of this sort that deal with very important future events. There are persons who have experienced dreams of this kind. We know that even the most intellectual people cannot predict the future. Yet as one sleeps, the future has from time to time been spelled out for one. How does this happen? Where do these dreams come from? The Bible tells us that God can speak to us in dreams and through visions of the night. When we are at times confused or troubled about things, God can inform us of what He wants us to know. Job 33: 15–16 states, "In a dream, in a vision of the night, when deep sleep falleth upon men, in slumberings upon the bed; then he openeth the ears of men, and sealeth their instruction."

That is exactly what happened to King Nebuchadnezzar. Yet when he awakened the next morning, he could not remember his dream. This, of course, happens to us all. Often I know that I have dreamed something during the night, and the next day I cannot remember it. Yet a mere word from someone may trigger off something, and what I have dreamed the night before comes back to me. We have all had such experiences.

Asking the Impossible?

But King Nebuchadnezzar was very disturbed and troubled by the dream he could not remember. So he called all the wise men, along with the magicians, the astrologers, the sorcerer, and the Chaldeans and ordered that they tell him the dream and its interpretation. He said, "I have dreamed a dream and my spirit was troubled to know the dream." Then the Chaldeans said to the king, "O King, live for ever: tell thy servants the dream, and we will show the interpretation." But Nebuchadnezzar could not remember the dream, so he said, "The thing is gone from me: if ye will not make known unto me the dream, with the interpretation thereof, ye shall be cut in pieces, and your houses shall be made a dunghill." They were dumbstruck! Then the Chaldeans answered the king, "There is not a man upon the earth that can show the king's matter." This angered the king and he became furious. He commanded that all the wise men throughout Babylon be killed. Arioch, the captain of the king's guards, was therefore sent to slay the wise men.

Obviously, Daniel was not there during this time of turmoil. But when he heard of the king's command, he met with the captain, and the both of them went to the king, where Daniel showed him the dream with the interpretation.

Now from this story of Daniel and King Nebuchadnezzar, I would like to take two sentences that I think are of importance to us. First, verse 10 tells us: "There is not a man upon the earth that can show the king's matter." This is the statement of the wise men of Babylon. Secondly, verse 28 states: "But there is a God in heaven that revealeth secrets, and maketh known to the king Nebuchadnezzar what shall be in the latter days. Thy dream, and the visions of thy head upon thy bed, are these." This is the affirmation of Daniel.

Human Limitations

The statement of the wise men of Babylon: "There is not a man upon the earth that can show . . ." The king had asked for the dream and the interpretation of the dream. He was told that no man on earth could do such a thing. Here is an open recognition of man's weakness and powerlessness. The men who made the statement to the king were intelligent men, yet they were powerless to help the king.

This is a rather pessimistic statement. It has a discouraging note. To be caught up in hard times and conditions with grave problems and then to be told that no man on earth can help you or save you is discouraging to say the least. It is depressing to say to a sick man, for example, that there is no one who can help or heal his illness. How can one bear such a statement? The burden is too heavy. It dashes to the ground any hope that there might be.

But this statement of the wise men is so true – even today with so many scientific and medical discoveries. Man is still powerless

80

in many things. Even with the great discovery of heart transplants, man cannot change the heart. In other words, you cannot replace hate with love.

The wickedness, the violence, the cruelties in our world today surround us constantly, and man is seemingly powerless to do anything about it. Man is limited to his own power. He can comfort, but cannot give rest; he can give momentary joy, but not true happiness. Solomon says, "Even in laughter, the heart is sorrowful" (Proverbs 14: 13). We can grant to others honours, titles, riches, but never true life itself. We can govern the earth, but we cannot govern our own life. Ecclesiastes 8: 8 says: "There is no man that hath the power over the spirit to retain the spirit; neither hath the power in the day of death." Yes, in many things, the wise men in the world today – whether they be doctor, lawyer, politician, or even the leader of a great nation – all must declare and confess that "there is no man upon the earth that can do this." There is no man that has the power to forgive sins, nor to change the human heart. Maybe there are some who do not agree with this and do not want to hear it. But it is the truth! Of course, I have no wish to push you into despair, but you *must* see the reality of the thing. The statement is pessimistic, without hope, *but it is true.*

Someone may come to me and ask, "How then can my daughter, my children, my husband, be saved?" One thing is certain, they cannot and will not be saved by man. Salvation is not in the power of man, it rests only in God through Jesus Christ our Lord who spilled His precious blood on Calvary. This now leads us to see:

God's limitless Dimensions

The affirmation of Daniel: "But there is a God in heaven . . . "
In Babylon the tension was high. There seemed to be no salvation for the wise men. They had proved powerless. But when the king ordered the slaying of these men, Daniel went to the king and asked for the execution to be delayed. In doing this he promised Nebuchadnezzar that he would interpret the dream. Then he went to his three companions, the Hebrew children, and encouraged them, saying that the mercies of God most High would be with them. They would not perish with the others.

81

We do not know how long they prayed – one day, two, three? And we do not know whether they just prayed or whether they fasted too, as in the days of Queen Esther. But we do know that God answered their prayers and revealed to them the secret of the dream. Daniel then went with Arioch to the king and repeated the statement made by the wise men. He said, "The secret which the king has demanded the wise men, the astrologers, the magicians, the soothsayers cannot show unto the king." Daniel thus confirmed the powerlessness of man. Then Daniel continued, saying: "But there is a God in heaven that revealeth secrets." What a wonderful truth this is! Today, when man has been proved powerless to face some of the critical problems found in the world, and the life of man seems to hang by a thread, let us not forget that there is a God in heaven who can do wonders.

I want this marvellous truth to be known to everyone. It was stated long ago by a servant of God who lived a pure life and kept himself away from sin. He walked with God and understood God's ways. Moreover, he was inspired by the Spirit of God. Therefore, his word is trustworthy.

This Is Good News

This is truly good news for all men, believers and non-believers alike. All of you who are faced with critical problems, troubles, turmoils, trials; even though there is no man on earth who can help, remember, God surely can. Yes, even you who are ruined by sin, ruined physically and spiritually; you who are wretched, troubled, and feel hopeless, this is truly good news for you. There is a God that loves and cares for you. He will never leave you nor forsake you even in your darkest moment. Just have faith enough that God will bring you through. Are you in a situation when not even those who love you, nor your beloved friends who may even weep for you, can help you? Oh, then, lift up your eyes, for there is a God who can do anything. Never forget that though the witness of the wise men from Babylon still stands – there is no man on earth who can do this – Daniel's testimony is also true: there is a God in heaven *who can*. Remember that with God nothing is impossible. In Psalms 50: 15 we read: "Call upon me in the day of trouble: I will deliver thee, and thou shalt glorify me." Oh, how we need this mercy when we are troubled or under strained circumstances! Then the mercy of God is like a beacon in the darkest night.

Several years ago, in a large city, there was a terrible earthquake. While the houses and buildings were tumbling to destruction and people in panic were running for their lives, out of a church came the harmonious music of a song: "Rock of Ages, cleft for me, let me hide myself in Thee . . ." In these moments of panic, the organist tried to direct everyone's mind to the Rock of Ages where the children of men can find shelter in the time of storm. Never before had the organ had more value and given more inspiration than during that terrible moment. When everyone had apparently lost all hope, then the words of that song guided the distraught people to the only true escape from danger.

A Timeless Principle

Now this great principle applies to all times, Nebuchadnezzar's and ours. While all the scholars lost all sense of hope, and while Arioch was talking about death, Daniel had that ray of hope; there is a God in heaven. This good news lighted up the black night of despair. It was glorious good news to the frightened people who were waiting for death to come.

So for us! When there is no one to help, remember Daniel's words: there is a God in heaven, a God who is able to answer even the humanly impossible wish of Nebuchadnezzar. Yes, there is a God who can do anything. And through the centuries hundreds and thousands of experiences confirm Daniel's statement. People have called upon Him for help countless times through countless years, and in return have received wonderful blessings.

But not only have individual people learned this; so have entire nations. Israel, the chosen people, had such an opportunity. During Jehoshaphat's time, the Amorites declared war against Israel. A messenger came to King Jehoshaphat saying, "There cometh a great multitude against thee from beyond the sea on this side of Syria." And in 2 Chronicles 20: 3 we read: "Jehoshaphat feared, and set himself to seek the Lord, and proclaimed a fast throughout all Judah." In his prayer he said, "O our God, we have no might against this great company that cometh against us; neither know we what to do; but our eyes are upon thee." After he prayed, Zechariah came to him bringing God's answer: "Be not afraid, nor dismayed by reason of this great multitude; for the battle is not yours, but God's. Tomorrow go out against them for ye shall not need to fight in this battle; set yourselves, stand ye still, and see the salvation of the Lord with you." Indeed, on that critical day Jehoshaphat saw the great salvation of God.

O my dear brothers and sisters, Romanian brethren, learn this truth. Do not ever lose your hopes, not during the most trying times, not even when man shall say that there is no one who can help. Trust in this powerful, all-wise God! Call upon Him when you need Him most! And you will find that He can do anything. This is the greatest truth of all: *There is a God in heaven.*

The testimony of Jesus

Petru Popovici

Acts 1: 8; Revelation 19: 10

*But you shall receive power when the Holy Spirit
has come upon you; and you shall be my witnesses
in Jerusalem and in all Judea and Samaria and
to the end of the earth.*

*Then I fell down at his feet to worship him, but
he said to me, "You must not do that! I am a
fellow servant with you and your brethren who hold
the testimony of Jesus. Worship God." For the
testimony of Jesus is the spirit of prophecy.*

Christ the Lord is asking us to be witnesses for Him; not lawyers,
not defendants, but witnesses. This is the prime service He left
for His followers to do.

What Is a Witness's Task?

A Christian witness, of course, has something to say. And it is
very interesting that in the first century it was recognised that
the *message* they had to bear was *a message with a note of
shame and of reproach.* They had to talk about One who was
sentenced to death and crucified. They had to testify about One
who was despised, about One who was spat upon, about One
who was scourged, about One who had to die as the worst of
the thieves. Now, think a little! How extremely difficult it would
be to go and tell people that message. Is it even possible to go
with such a message? Do you realize what scorn would be
attracted? Even the children would laugh about your Hero. With
such a message do you want to conquer the world?

It is really true, as I have said, that the message had a real note of shame. But it has always been so, and Christ's followers have no other message, even today. This we must never forget. The apostle Paul said to the Corinthians (1 Cor. 1: 18), "For the preaching of the cross is to them that perish foolishness; but unto us which are saved it is the power of God." He goes on in verse 22: "For the Jews require a sign, and the Greeks seek after wisdom: But we preach Christ crucified, unto the Jews a stumbling-block, and unto the Greeks foolishness; but unto them which are called, both Jews and Greeks, Christ the power of God, and the wisdom of God." The apostles and disciples went into the world with this message only. And even though it has a central note of reproach, they started to turn the world upside down. And when we today are willing to bear that shame and reproach, we too can turn the world upside down.

A Message of Life

But on the other hand, this *message has a note of glory*. Christ Himself put it on their lips when He said, "For God so loved the world that he gave his only begotten son, that whosoever believeth in him should not perish, but have everlasting life" (John 3: 16). The apostle Peter emphasizes this fact in his letters. It is a message of glory! 1 Peter 2: 24 states, "Who his own self bare our sins in his own body on the tree, that we, being dead to sins, should live unto righteousness; by whose stripes ye were healed." Yes, it is true that we preach Christ *crucified*, but not *just* crucified. There was a real purpose in it all. He was crucified *for you and me*. He died in our place. He suffered our punishment, and that in order that we can have eternal salvation. Others may scorn us. Others may not understand. But we have no other message than Christ and Him crucified – and it is the message of life.

The apostle Paul projects the same note of glory. He says, "This is a faithful saying, and worthy of all acceptation, that Christ Jesus came into the world to save sinners; of whom I am chief" (1 Tim. 1: 15). In 1 John 4: 14 we read, "We have seen and do testify that the Father sent the Son to be the Saviour of the world."

In the light of this, therefore, we are to be witnesses for Christ,

86

telling all the world that He came down to save. John says, "That which was from the beginning, which we have heard, which we have seen with our eyes, which we have looked upon, and our hands have handled, of the Word of life; for the life was manifested, and we have seen it, and bear witness and shew unto you that eternal life, which was with the Father and was manifested unto us; that which we have seen and heard declare we unto you" (1 John 1: 1–3). We have no other message. For others, it may well be a message of foolishness, but for us it is a message of a glorious new life. The crucified Christ is the Saviour of the world. He has made us free from the guilt of sin and from its penalty.

The disciples went out to conquer the world for Christ without any weapon save the message of salvation. O, message of sacrifice, how great the need of you in this guilty world! O, message of Divine love, you are so necessary in a world of hate! O, message of holy peace, you are so essential in an agitated world! Welcome among us, you are a message of power.

And you, followers of Jesus, bear everywhere this blessed message! You, blind men healed by Christ, be witnesses for Him! You, lepers cleansed by Jesus, be witnesses for Him! You, men from Gadara, possessed with devils but delivered by Christ, be witnesses for Him! You, dumb men whose tongues were loosed, speak for Jesus, be witnesses for Him! O, all sinners, who deserved to be crucified for your guilt, but Jesus took your place on the cross and now you are forgiven, be witnesses for Him. Tell to the world that Christ is willing to receive and to forgive even the chief of sinners – anyone who will repent as did the thief on the cross.

> Tell the world there is a Saviour
> Who fulfills his every claim;
> He is able to deliver
> All who call upon His Name.

Are You Saved?

Among the readers of this message, there are surely some whose sins are not forgiven, those who have not received the wonderful peace of God, who do not have that sweet rest which only Christ can give. I testify to all of you who do not have Christ in your life, that Jesus has the power to forgive sins; He has the power to change radically your life; He is able to give you a wonderful peace. And "when He giveth quietness, who then can make trouble?" (Job 34: 29). I know this from my own experience. I know He is able. It is like a man suffering from a serious disease, but then wonderfully cured by a physician.

That is what Christ can do, and I want to tell all who are spiritually sick about that Physician; I want to tell all people about Jesus Christ, my Saviour. I was sick with the illness of sin, but He healed me completely. When nobody else could help, then He came and met my need. I tell you that Jesus is a wonderful and great Physician and He is able to heal you just now. What a blessed hour! How precious and unforgettable it is. I came to Christ crucified and He poured out on me His amazing grace; my sins were washed away by His blood and my life was regenerated by His Holy Spirit. I was lost, but He "found" me. He is a wonderful Saviour. I know this from my own life. He is able and willing to save you also. Come to Him right now!

The Power of Christ

Now, let me direct your thoughts to *the power* available for serving Christ as a witness. It demands great power. You disciples of Christ, you who have the message of Jesus, do you want to conquer the world for Him? Do you realize what it means? Do you think that you will be able to conquer the entire world for Christ? Do you have the power for such a battle: Are we not all so often like the disciples on the night of betrayal? Don't we often forsake Him and flee away just as they did? You, Peter, do you want to conquer the world for Christ? But you were not ready to tell a servant girl that you are a disciple of Jesus! While Jesus was on trial in the judgment hall and the high priest interrogating Him, outside you denied Him. Your place was inside, in the judgment hall, to give witness for Jesus before the the high priest. But you did not have the power, so you began to curse and to swear that you did not know Him. Now you want to conquer the world for Christ! It is possible? Oh, yes, *it is possible*. Paul, the apostle of the Gentiles, gives us the answer. He says, "God hath chosen the foolish things of the world to confound the wise; and God has chosen the weak things of the world to confound the things which are mighty. And base things of the world, and the things which are despised, hath God chosen, yea, and things which are not, to bring to nought things that are" (1 Cor. 1: 27, 28).

"All right," we say, "I am weak, despised, nothing. But how can I find power to witness?" Christ Himself has given the answer: "Ye shall receive power, after that the Holy Spirit is come upon you; and ye shall be witnesses unto me, both in Jerusalem, and in all Judea, and in Samaria, and unto the uttermost part of the earth" (Acts 1: 8).

Christ desires that we all come to understand that it is not by human power that we may conquer the world for Him, but by the *power of His Spirit*. The Apostle Paul says, "Who goeth to warfare any time at his own charges?" (1 Cor. 9: 7). That small group of early disciples had not the power nor the money nor the means in order to fulfill the great commandment to preach the gospel. They were powerless, but in the name of all disciples, Paul shouts from prison: "I can do all things through Christ which strengtheneth me" (Phil. 4: 13). Yes, the power of Jesus was enough for them – and it is enough for us in our day; in our kind of world with all its problems.

This power for witness was proved in their life. I want to make it clear that the unmeasured power of the Holy Spirit was given for nothing else, except to bear the testimony of Jesus. All the gifts of the Holy Spirit, all the fruits and miracles, were for this primary purpose. And they became witnesses because they had received the power of the Holy Spirit. What a wonderful power! Now they are speaking as never before. When Jesus chose them He said, "Ye shall be brought before governors and kings for my sake, for a testimony against them and the Gentiles. But when they deliver you up, take no thought how or what ye shall speak . . . for it is not ye that speak, but the Spirit of your Father which speaketh in you" (Matt. 10: 18–20).

When Peter and John were arrested and brought before the Sanhedrin because of their testimony for Jesus, they were not afraid; they were not trembling. They spoke with a great boldness. When the Sanhedrin commanded them not to speak at all nor teach in the name of Jesus, Peter and John answered, "Whether it be right in the sight of God to hearken unto you more than unto God, judge ye" (Acts 4: 18–19).

The Sanhedrin took note of this "power". The disciples were not silent but boldly proclaimed the love of God in Christ. The world hated them for it, as the world hates us now. But Jesus demonstrated then *and now* through His people His great power. He said to His disciples, "If the world hate you, ye know that it hated me before it hated you. If ye were of the world, the world would love his own: but because ye are not of the world, but I have chosen you out of the world, therefore the world hateth you. Remember the word that I said unto you: The servant is not greater than his lord. If they have persecuted me, they will also persecute you" (John 15: 18–20). "These things have I spoken unto you, that you should not be offended . . . And these things will they do unto you, because they have not known the Father, nor me" (John 16: 1, 3).

The disciples were not of the world, therefore the world hated them. And through the centuries the true Christians have been a puzzle to the world. Do you think that we are understood today? No, even though we are living in a civilized world, a world which has so many ways of searching the phenomenon of the nature of things. With all its knowledge and discernment, the world cannot search out the phenomenon of the new life in Jesus Christ our Lord. We Christians are, therefore, "unknown" to the world. Many think that we are against the culture of our age. But our children are the best students in schools and university. Others say that we are against modern developments such as the technological advances of our day. But this is not true. Although just a small minority of our Christian people have radios, for example, this not because they are against the radio, but they are just too poor and do not have the money to buy a radio. Because we left the Orthodox Church, some say that we left the faith of our fathers, that now we are without God, that we have gone astray. The truth is that we have only gone astray from sin. Prior to our conversion, we were without God, but now we are living in faith. We are unknown by the world. They just do not understand our new life in Christ.

For the disciples of Christ, it was not so important that the world did not know them; but they were vitally concerned that the world should come to know Jesus their Master. Against the church which was at Jerusalem a great persecution broke out. They were all scattered abroad throughout the regions of Judea and Samaria, except the apostles. God provoked them to be witnesses for Christ wherever this persecution drove them. In such a time, some of them perhaps wanted to be silent – but they could not.

Do you remember that Jonah wanted to be silent? Remember how he paid the passage fare on a ship to run from God. He went down into the hold of the ship and went fast asleep. But there was a storm and an amazing awakening for old Jonah. He must be a witness and do God's will. He was provoked to speak.

Stephen, too, was provoked to give his testimony – and today it happens the same way. Many Christians are provoked to be witnesses for Christ. It is impossible to be silent. Christ fulfilled His promise; He gave to His followers a power of speaking the things of the gospel.

Witnessing Without Words

Moreover, the Holy Spirit gave them a Christlike life. This was a witness without words. He who bears a lantern, a light in the darkness, does not have to cry, "I have a lantern." The light has its own "voice", and those who have the Light of the World in their life bear a powerful testimony. A clean and pure life in a sinful, dark world is a blessed witness. The apostle Paul says, "We have this treasure in earthen vessels, that the excellency of the power may be of God, and not of us . . . For we which live are always delivered unto death for Jesus' sake, that the life also of Jesus might be made manifest in our mortal flesh" (2 Cor. 4: 7, 11). They, having Christ in them, were witnesses for Him.

It is true that the world never gave up the struggle against the new-born church. In Revelation 12: 17 we read, "And the dragon was wroth with the woman, and went to make war with the remnant of her seed, which keep the commandments of God, and have the testimony of Jesus Christ." What a savage war it was! But in all their persecutions and terrible sufferings, they received power to stay faithful and to be more than conquerors. Further, they were witnesses for Christ by enduring torture and suffering. The Christians of the first centuries endured with joy all their trials. Paul says, "I Paul am made a minister; who now

91

rejoice in my sufferings for you, and fill up that which is behind of the afflictions of Christ in my flesh for his body's sake, which is the church" (Col. 1: 23, 24).

Yes, Christ promised and He has given power for witness through speech, through living and through sufferings. Undefeated by the power of the devil, they were witnesses for Christ, facing the hate of the world, and they arrived in glory. In Revelation 6: 9 John tells us that he has seen under the altar the souls of them that were slain for the word of God and for the testimony which they held. What a wonderful testimony! Through their lives they confessed the love of Christ and through their death they demonstrated their love to Christ. Today's world needs such witnesses, Christians who are full of power.

The Results of a Faithful Witness

Now, let me tell you how this testimony, in the power of the Holy Spirit, produced such a blessed effect. First, their testimony for Jesus had a blessed effect upon all who were enslaved by sin. They were thirsty for deliverance, for salvation. For them the gospel was truly good news. They came to know Christ and to receive His salvation.

Secondly, their testimony had a blessed effect upon those who were indifferent. At that time many people lived quite carelessly in regard to eternity. But they were awakened; they realized they were sinful men, that they needed a Saviour and that Jesus alone can save. This testimony had a tremendous effect upon careless people.

Something more: the testimony for Christ had a shaking effect even upon their enemies. Many of them came to realize how useless their actions were, like the Pharisees described in John 12: 19: "The Pharisees therefore said among themselves, perceive ye how ye prevail nothing? Behold, the world is gone after him." In other words, you tried to hinder the world from coming to Christ, but don't you see that your effort is in vain? The testimony of Jesus had a great effect not only in that the Pharisees came to see how useless their persecution was, but also that it was actually having an opposite effect. The Christians, instead of becoming less and less in number due to being persecuted, were actually increasing in number. Tertullian in writing to the emperor said,

"Even those who were hating the Christians, they themselves became Christians and now they are hating what they were doing before. We are only very young, but already we fill your empire, your citadels, the islands, the fortresses, the houses, the fields, the tribes, the palace, the senate, the square, and we have left you nothing except your pagan temples. Our number is constantly increasing. And it does so even more when you try to destroy us. The seed is the blood of the Christians." The enemies wanted to extinguish the heavenly fire. They started a storm, hoping to blow it out, but as in the summer fields, the fire burns better when it is blown by the wind. So it is with this spiritual fire. If there is no wind, the fire burns in a small place and then dies out; but if there is the wind to blow, it spreads with great speed and covers whole areas.

Satan wanted this holy fire of the divine love to die out, but only succeeded in cheating himself. Oh demons, oh cruel kings, executioners, torturers of the Christians through the centuries, you thought that you could extinguish the testimony for Jesus. Yet you never realized that you, through your horrible means, would actually contribute to the spreading of this testimony of Jesus!

Another effect was the conversion of many enemies. Saul of Tarsus was officially charged with the persecution of Christians. But Saul was converted, and this "enemy of Christ" became an apostle of Christ. Christian history has many such cases. For example, the apostle Paul wrote to Titus about a Christian named Zenas, a lawyer. We do not know how he was converted to Christ. It is possible that he was present at the trials of the Christians, listening to their testimony and seeing their faces. Maybe this moved him. At any rate, he was converted to Christ. As a lawyer he knew that a witness may well lie for money or to save his life. Yet here were Christians, testifying unashamedly and bravely that they were believers, knowing full well that by doing so they would be sentenced to death. They would rather die than lie or deny their faith. This obviously demonstrated that they had received something better. Even a criminal, when he realizes that there is no way out, may confess that he is guilty. Now what kind of men are these, that when the judge asks them to say they are not Christians, courageously affirm, "We are Christians!"? They hold fast their testimony until death. This kind of testimony is an obvious demonstration to all that their faith was real and grounded in genuine truth.

Tertullian in his *Apologeticum* tells the judge: "A man cries out: I am Christian! But you seem to want to hear what he is not. You put the Christian through tortures, to draw out the truth. He confesses he is a Christian. Nevertheless, you still torture him. If he would deny the faith, you would believe him. In some strange way, you consider the Christian guilty of all iniquities and you torment him so as to elicit a denial of arrest in order to deliver him from punishment, out of which you cannot deliver him if he does not deny the faith. You want him to deny that he is guilty in order to declare him innocent, and this without his will and without any guilt in his past."

Yes, the judge wanted to force the Christians to deny their testimony. But they utterly failed, and God's people carried their faith in Christ to the uttermost part of the world with wonderful effect. I ask you: Where are the idols of old heathen worship? Where are they? They lie in the dust of the ground. How were they defeated? Through the testimony of Jesus Christ. This is the means by which the followers of Jesus can conquer the world.

Become a Witness Now

My brethren, I deeply desire that you too become witnesses for Christ and that your testimony will have a blessed effect. You can conquer the world for Christ through your testimony, and you yourself will enter into the glory of the Lord. In Revelation 15: 2 we read, "And I saw as it were a sea of glass mingled with fire: and them that had gotten the victory over the beast, and over his image and over his mark, and over the number of his name, stand on the sea of glass, having the harps of God". Also in chapter 12, verse 11: "They overcame him by the blood of the Lamb, and by the word of their testimony, and they loved not their lives unto the death." "And after these things I heard a great voice of much people in heaven, saying, Alleluia; salvation, and glory, and honour, and power, unto the Lord our God" (Rev. 19: 1).

The disciples of Christ have been witnesses for Christ throughout the world. Follow in their footsteps. Day by day bear the testimony of Jesus through your words, through your living and through your enduring of all trials for His glory. Amen.

Alexander G. Balc

The Reverend Dr Alexander G. Balc was born on April 19, 1912, in the town of Diosig, Romania. His father was a deacon of the Baptist church, his mother, now over eighty, is still serving God in the Romanian church.

Baptized on his confession of faith at the age of thirteen, Alexander started his first preaching at nineteen. He studied in Italy, Romania and later in the USA, graduating from two universities in law and business administration, and finally obtaining his doctorate in divinity and human relations, specializing in the study of ecclesiastical law.

After ordination he served in the Baptist Church of Jassy, Romania, and in other churches. He was also a representative of the Baptist people in the Romanian Union, being a member of the Union's Department of Education and Publicity. He has attended congresses of the Baptist World Alliance as a member of the official delegation and president of the Romanian Young People's Organization.

In the second world war, as an officer in the Romanian army, he was awarded the highest decorations of the country: the Romanian Crown and the Romanian Star. In recent years Dr Balc has travelled to the United States and is now serving the Romanian Baptist Church of Akron, Ohio.

This message was delivered first (on the "Day of Elijah", July 20, as celebrated in Romanian churches) at a Baptist Convention held in the region of Moldova, with the assembled people from many localities.

Confrontation on Mount Carmel

Alexander G. Balc

1 Kings 18: 21, 30, 39

And Elijah came near to all the people, and said,
"How long will you go limping with two different
opinions? If the Lord is God, follow him; but if
Baal, then follow him." And the people did not
answer him a word . . . Then Elijah said to all the
people; "Come near to me;" and all the people
came near to him. And he repaired the altar of
the Lord that had been thrown down; . . . and when
all the people saw it, they fell on their faces; and
they said, "The Lord, he is God; the Lord, he is
God."

Dear brothers and friends in Jesus Christ!

From the ranks of God's mighty men, one of the most illustrious is a man called Elijah the Tishbite. He was an inhabitant of Gilead. This is how the Scriptures present him in the book of Kings.

All believers look to him as the "prophet of fire". Among our Romanian people, he is thought of with awe. This is probably the reason why he has been given a special day in our ecclesiastical calendars, like this twentieth day of July. Others honour his life and ministry by giving their beloved children his name.

On the occasion of this service, I trust we shall grasp an understanding of this faithful son and servant of God. We want to learn something of his personality and attempt to understand his mission, and certainly we wish to share with him his victory on Mount Carmel.

Setting the Stage

The appearance of Elijah in the pages of the biblical history is sudden and dramatic. The events recorded in 1 Kings occurred almost three thousand years ago on the Mountain of Carmel in the region of Samaria in old Palestine, and they represent a most powerful and graphic manifestation of living and active faith. Elijah above all was one who believed and trusted in Almighty God.

In the account given to us in the Scriptures, we see all the tragedy of man departed and estranged from his creator God. At the same time, however, there is presented the courageous and powerful affirmation of a sincere, fearless, faithful man, ready to face any kind of risk – even that of a wicked king – so that the proper worship of God in the lives of the people might be re-established. The people's defection from God had brought misery upon the whole nation. And Elijah was there to end the tragedy.

The figure of Elijah, appearing in history as one raising his voice against idolatry, is pictured as the epitome of virtue, power, authority and commitment to God. The herald of Carmel seemingly does not know fear. There are no compromises which could cloud the impact of the divine Word on his lips. So, in this spirit, he starts his confrontation with the king, the prophets of Baal and the people.

But something of this same spirit is common to all the great servants of God. It is seen in the life of Moses, the great legislator of God's people Israel; in the life of Joshua, the worthy successor of Moses; also in the lives of Gideon, Daniel, John the Baptist, and Paul, along with the endless ranks of the saints of God. All whom God mightily used bore the mark of commitment to God. And hence they kept awake the consciences of men and directed them into the way that is pleasing to God and thus toward a happy life on the earth and ultimately to heaven itself.

All these men of God rose to the challenge to face the whole world with the message expressed by the apostle Paul: "Now then we are ambassadors for Christ, as though God did beseech you by us: we pray you in Christ's stead, be ye reconciled to God" (2 Cor. 5: 20).

The Confrontation

The principles of the confrontation on Carmel that motivated Elijah the prophet were well justified. Among these might be mentioned the following:

1. The rebellious departing from God and from the true worship of God by the whole Israelite nation;

2. Replacing the true worship of God with idolatry and sinful service toward strange gods who had no life;

3. The broken-down altar of the Lord, that which was once erected for the glory of God;

4. The duality of loyalty and spiritual blindness of the people, graphically verbalized by the prophet when he asked, "How long halt ye between two opinions?"

What must be seen as primary in God's man Elijah is his trust and commitment to the guidance of God. And the secret of this guidance is found in his prayer life. Listen to how he prayed: "Lord, God of Abraham, Isaac, and of Israel, let it be known this day that thou art God in Israel, and that I am thy servant, and that I have done all these things at thy word" (1 Kings 18: 36).

Before Elijah arrived at Carmel, however, he passed through a wonderful experience. Actually, the experience prepared him for the encounter he was to have with the prophets of Baal in the near future. Through the secret believer, Obadiah, Elijah revealed himself to Ahab the King: "Behold, Elijah is here!" (1 Kings 18: 11).

Now look at the events of the meeting between a King – and an evil one at that – and a humble servant of God! Of course, many times sincere believers and servants of God have had to stand before leaders and authorities. Facing trials and judgment for one's faith in God and the Saviour Christ Jesus is not new. But it is then that the truth of the Scriptures, with its promise that they need not fear what they should say because words would be given them, becomes a very marvellous promise.

Catch the drama of the scene at the meeting of the angry,

frustrated king, and the man of God. The king wished to get rid of Elijah once and for all. Ahab addresses the prophet and says, "Art thou he that troubleth Israel?"

But then look at the fearlessness of Elijah. He turns off the king's accusation and by the virtue of his divine power and authority he confronts the king and charges him, saying: "I have not troubled Israel; but thou, and thy father's house, in that ye have forsaken the commandments of the Lord, and thou hast followed Baalim" (1 Kings 18: 18).

This is the indictment Elijah hurls at King Ahab. And here is the ground for the victory on Carmel. Here is the real confrontation. If Elijah can stand his ground here, he can stand it any place, including Mount Carmel. If he can render a right judgment here, he can do it wherever he is. And stand his ground he did.

So when the final issue arose at Mount Carmel, it was evident who would be proved right, on whose side the truth settled. Elijah had been well prepared and thus proved a worthy advocate of the cause of his God. He became a good defender of the work committed to him; and before God and before the king and the people he wrought a great victory for the name of Israel's God.

The natural geographical beauty of Mount Carmel is attractive and pleasant. But that is not what makes Carmel great. Much more than the beauty of the spot is the fact that there God gave a powerful affirmation of His own existence. He showed unmistakably that He can answer the prayers of His children; that He is able to keep them faithful; that His divine hands lead His own through the troubles that ensue as a result of confrontation with the world; and that wonderful victory can be achieved through faith.

We thank God that when there are men, kings and leaders, who attempt to lead people into spiritual blindness, to estrange them from God, there are also prophets like Elijah, men working for God and His great cause in the world. These are the ambassadors for Christ and for His gospel; witnesses who believe and are committed into the hands of the One who declared: "All power is given unto me in heaven and in earth. Go ye therefore, and teach all nations, baptizing them in the name of the Father, and of the Son, and of the Holy Ghost: teaching them to observe all things whatsoever I have commanded you: and lo,

I am with you alway, even unto the end of the world" (Matt. 28: 18–20).

The Prophet's Insightful Actions

Now we cannot overlook the manner and the wisdom of this prophet of Carmel. Here one can discern the clear guidance and wisdom of God.

Please observe, my beloved brothers and friends in Christ, that after Elijah proclaimed judgment to the king, he went up to Carmel. There he called to himself the king and all the people. He further summoned all the 450 priests of Baal and the 400 of Astarte who were fed at the table of Jezebel.

Elijah established first the circumstances that must surround the confrontation. He chose as the means of the trial, the sacrifice, that which plays a determinative role in the lives of men. According to the principle involved in any sacrificial system, it is known to whom the sacrifice is brought and to whom it is offered. If the sacrifice is "accepted", then here is where reality exists. But if there is no answer to the sacrifice, no answering voice to prayer, that means that something is wrong, basically and tragically wrong. Thus if a man cries and calls on the name of his Baal from morning until night, if there is no voice, no answer, all that has been done is in vain, useless and without merit. This was the setting of the stage for the great confrontation between God and Baal.

And it is not different in principle today. If you see in your life some aspect of contemporary idolatry, and if you experience in your life the same sort of rejection to your prayers of need, with no voice or answer, then it may well be that you are living without God and far from His purpose and will. Let me put before you at this time the same challenge which Israel faced on the top of Mount Carmel: "How long halt ye between two opinions? If the Lord be God, follow Him!" How long the Lord's altars have been broken down; broken down in the lives of individuals, families, contemporary society, and much more, even in the churches from which the Spirit of Christ has departed. How long, I ask again, will the altars remain without acceptable sacrifices, in ruins and broken down? Oh, the tragedy of altars on which the sacred fire of the sacrifice has gone out and all is cold and lifeless! But now, back to the biblical account.

100

God's Man Prepares

God's man first dressed the altars. What a beautiful thing! And what commitment! To be a builder of the Lord's altars is a wonderful service. It is true worship. It is surely much more preferable than to be among those who neglect the altars of the Lord, even though there is a price to pay.

After the altars were dressed, Elijah started to pray. It was a simple prayer but full of power and faith; full of trust in God that his prayer will be heard and answered.

Listen to this prayer from his heart: "Hear me, O Lord, hear me, that this people may know that thou art the Lord God, and that thou hast turned their heart back again." The result of fervent prayer? "Then the fire of the Lord fell, and consumed the burnt sacrifice and the wood, and the stones, and the dust, and licked up the water that was in the trench" (1 Kings 18:38). And the result of God's actions to answered prayer? "And when all the people saw it, they fell on their faces; and they said, 'The Lord he is God; the Lord, he is the God'" (v. 39). When God's power falls and His presence is made known, evil is always routed.

". . . Elijah said unto them, 'Take the prophets of Baal, let not one of them escape.' And they took them: and Elijah brought them down to the brook Kishon, and slew them there" (v. 40). The confrontation was over, and God's name was vindicated.

The Truth of the Confrontation

Now the contest on Carmel can be seen as something of a picture of the coming judgment promised in the Word of God. It is a very serious issue. The day is coming when all mankind will stand before God and all evil will finally be dealt with. This we must all understand. God's word is clear on the issue.

Therefore, I would end my message today, saying to all who want to be pleasing to God and to be sure of the promised rewards of heaven, remember the words of Amos, God's prophet who called out long ago, but today calls us with the same appeal: ". . . Prepare to meet thy God, O Israel." Oh, won't you receive God's sacrifice of Calvary so as to be prepared? That is the *only* way to be prepared for that great judgment day. I beg you to trust God's perfect sacrifice, in Christ's precious name. Do it now!   Amen.

101

Sermons from
HUNGARY

Andreas Herjeczki

The Reverend Andreas Herjeczki was born on November 7, 1919, in Vegegyhaza, a village on the great Panonian plain in Hungary. He was in the Baptist Theological Seminary in Budapest from 1941 to 1944. As a close friend said, his life was a "three-fold work of the Holy Spirit", the title of his sermon. In the predominantly Roman Catholic village of his birth, his mother was the first Baptist believer. Because of her conversion she suffered much from her husband and from her fanatical relatives. She could hardly read the Bible in her own home because of the pressure. Therefore, a friendly lady in the neighbourhood opened her home, and there in secret she read the Bible.

But God was in it all. It opened the way to establishing a small Baptist congregation in the village; and this godly mother, a weak woman, but with strong faith, preached the gospel for many years in the village. The truth preached in Pastor Herjeczki's sermon was realized; the Holy Spirit brought many to salvation through the work of her devoted life.

The mother, who suffered much, passed away in her forties. Like Hannah of the Bible she too wanted very much to raise up a son to be a servant of God. Andreas was born in 1919, and the battle started. Her relatives were eager to take the boy to the Roman Catholic church for baptism. The mother was against infant baptism. When the mother left home one day for a short time, her sister-in-law took advantage of the situation and put the little boy in the deep snow, believing that the baby without baptism was possessed by demons. But good-hearted neighbours took him in and saved the little one from freezing to death. The wise mother, afraid for her son, gave him to some relatives. They, in turn, went to a priest who baptized Andreas. In this time of darkness and fear, her heart yearned for her little son. She so wanted to see him as a servant of her Saviour and Lord.

One morning Andreas woke up hearing his mother praying: "Father in heaven, I am a weak woman. I do not know what more I could do for Thy kingdom. But here is my son. Take him and make him to be Thy servant – instead of me if need be." This prayer of his mother Andreas never forgot.

And it was not in vain. When the boy was twelve, he lost his mother. From that time many unhappy things occurred in his life. Like other boys, he too tried to find happiness in the world. But the faithful prayers of his mother reached him, and when he was nineteen the grace of God reached his heart and he came to salvation. From the first moment of his conversion, he was aware that he was to be a preacher of Christ and His wonderful gospel. The call came to him in the Scriptures: "Whom shall I send, and who will go for us?" (Is. 6: 8).

The Holy Spirit filled his heart, and he could not run away from his destiny. He offered his life to Jesus. Since that time he has been an ardent servant of the kingdom of God. His great desire is that he, his faithful wife, and their five children should be a proof of the three-fold work of the Holy Spirit. One of their sons is now engaged in theological study at the Baptist Theological Seminary in Budapest.

The three-fold work of the Holy Spirit

Andreas Herjeczki

John 14: 16–17

*And I will pray the Father, and he will give you
another Counsellor, to be with you for ever, even
the Spirit of truth, whom the world cannot receive,
because it neither sees him nor knows him; you
know him; for he dwells with you, and will be in you.*

By virtue of the death of our Lord Jesus Christ and His glorious
resurrection, the work of redemption was "finished"! This is an
accomplished fact. And all history attests to its validity and
finality. However, calling those who should be saved, thus gather-
ing the *ecclesia* and adorning the bride of Christ, is occurring
continually. This work is always taking place in all ages and
cultures. The calling task is being done by the Holy Spirit,
using His own instruments, the people of God. That is why, from
the point of view of salvation history, we call our age "the age of
the Spirit". We distinguish three phases in the work of the Spirit
of God. Prior to our conversion, He works *for us* that the life of
Jesus may be seen more and more. After conversion, He wishes
to work *in us and through us* in order to save others. Let us view
these works of the Holy Spirit in that order.

First, The Holy Spirit Works For Us.

In the beginning of every sound conversion, God's Spirit awakens
us in some way or other to a realization of our sins. He judges the
sin in us, showing us at the same time the abundant riches of the

107

forgiving grace of Jesus Christ. Every true believer can testify to his experience of how God's love sought and found him. I have never met a believer who would attribute his conversion to himself. Every genuine Christian testifies that his conversion was initiated by God. God broke into his life. Sometimes God invades the personality with a gentle paternal embrace, at other times by difficult circumstance. But God always works with the purpose of drawing the individual to Himself.

It is usually characteristic of such an experience that this work of the Holy Spirit can be seen only when looking back. There is no greater pleasure for the illuminated mind than, casting a retrospective glance back over the course of life, to contemplate with amazement God's work in our life and to praise God for His eternal Spirit by which He sought and accepted us as His children through faith. We are taught by the Holy Scripture that man is dead because of sin. But in something of the same way as the spring sunshine calls into life the sleeping flower buds, so the Holy Spirit gives life to the heart that is dead in sin. There is nothing more magnificent than experiencing this in our own life.

According to the apostle Paul if anyone in faith utters the words "Jesus is Lord", he does so by the Holy Spirit (1 Cor. 12: 3). When, however, someone hardens his heart and opposes or struggles against the testimony of Jesus Christ, he does so against the Holy Spirit. This is the reason Stephen the martyr said, "How stubborn you are! How heathen your hearts, how deaf you are to God's message! You are just like your ancestors: You too have always resisted the Holy Spirit!" (Acts 7: 51).

The Sin Against the Holy Spirit

Here the idea of the sin against the Holy Spirit begins to become more clear. Our Saviour said, "Anyone who says something against the Son of Man will be forgiven; but whoever says something against the Holy Spirit will not be forgiven – now or ever" (Matt. 12: 32). It is something of a mistake, of course, to think of some sins as being worse than others. Our Saviour never drew a horizontal line and said, "So far extends the forgiving grace of God *and no further*!" If it had been so, we could not preach on the text: "The blood of Jesus, His Son, makes us clean from *every sin*" (1 John 1: 7). We have to look for an explanation somewhere else.

108

Now if the sin against the Holy Spirit will never be forgiven, this is not because it exceeds the mercy of God's heart or the limit of His forgiving grace. Rather, it is because it carries *in itself* the reason for eternal judgment! Here is the point; we have seen that all conversions are the work of the Holy Spirit. If someone resists and rejects the promptings of the Holy Spirit who wants to save him and win him and thus offer forgiveness of sin through the blood of Jesus Christ, then it is impossible for him to come to Jesus so that God might save him. This is the same as attempting to save a drowning man who refuses to be saved by rejecting the only life-line thrown to him. "How shall we escape if we pay no attention to such a great salvation?" says the writer of Hebrews.

Thus, "As the Holy Spirit says, 'If you hear God's voice today. do not be stubborn' " (Heb. 3: 7–8). It is most dangerous to resist the work of the Holy Spirit that He performs for us.

But if we heed and come to Christ in repentance and faith, then:

The Holy Spirit Works in Us

There is only one place in the world where sinful man may meet God; at the foot of the cross of Calvary – on the footstool of repentance. When this happens, the Holy Spirit who has worked hitherto *for us*, begins His wonderful transforming work *in us*.

First of all, *He gives us new life.* "Flesh gives birth to flesh" (John 3: 6), and "What is made of flesh and blood cannot share in God's Kingdom" (1 Cor. 15: 50). "A man becomes an enemy of God when his mind is controlled by what human nature wants; for he does not obey God's law, and in fact he cannot obey it" (Rom. 8: 7), because he is dead on account of sin. It is the Spirit which gives life. "Spirit gives birth to Spirit" (John 3: 6), and we are born again. What a marvellous experience it is!

The Spirit Calls Us to Worship

Through the rebirth we become God's children – and at the same time citizens of heaven. "To show that you are his sons, God sent the Spirit of his Son into our hearts, the Spirit who cries "Father, my Father" (Gal. 4: 6). The believer's prayer does not consist of memorized phrases. Rather, it is a free flight and a pouring out of one's heart to the Heavenly Father. The Jews called God "The Lord of Hosts", "The Everlasting", "The Almighty". Jesus taught us to pray: "Our Father". This means that God is my father. This wonderful relationship was made possible by Jesus Christ, and the Holy Spirit makes it a living reality in our lives. When adoration arises in a believing heart, it is the Holy Spirit's flight towards God, leading us into genuine worship and praise.

The heart, which has been hitherto the home of sin, is transformed to become a temple of God. This is the magnificent teaching of the Holy Scripture. The almighty God, whom the heaven of heavens cannot contain, the footstool of whose feet is the earth, who does not live in temples made by hand, has been pleased to come to lowly mankind and to take habitation in believing hearts by the Holy Spirit. Is there any greater dignity in human experience than this? Notice, this includes no conditions. Wherever the Scriptures speak of it, they describe it as a natural consequence of being God's children. Jesus said, "You know him (the Holy Spirit) for he remains with you and lives in you" (John 14: 17). Paul said to the Corinthians, "Surely, you know that you are God's temple, and that God's Spirit lives in you (1 Cor. 3: 16). This is not a result of our human effort; this is God's gift given to us.

Moreover, He seals us unto the day of redemption. This also means that the day of our full redemption is not yet complete. Our mortal body is not yet redeemed from corruption. But it has been sealed by the Holy Spirit to the glory of Christ who will change our weak mortal bodies and make them like His own glorious body (Phil. 3: 21).

Finally, He makes our life overflowing. "On the last day of the feast Jesus stood up and said in a loud voice: 'As the Scripture says, "Whoever believes in me, streams of living water will pour out from his heart".' Jesus said this about the Spirit which those who believed in Him were about to receive" (John 7: 38–39). If the life in us is life indeed, and not merely affected piety, God will pour out the Holy Spirit upon us as the fragrance of flowers in spring. Life can be an overflowing life.

We have now reached the final great work of the Spirit. It comes full circle. In the same way as the Holy Spirit worked for me and in me, He will work through me for others.

The Holy Spirit Works Through Us

Our Lord Jesus Christ made the glorious promises: "Do not worry ahead of time about what you are going to say; when the time comes say whatever is given to you then. For the words you speak will not be yours, they will come from the Holy Spirit" (Mark 13: 11). Could there be any greater encouragement? Furthermore, "The Helper will come – the Spirit of truth, who comes from the Father. I will send him from the Father, and he will speak about me." But He does not speak without us, because our Saviour goes on to say, "And you too, will speak about me" (John 15: 26–27). Thus man becomes God's co-worker. It is a most wonderful thing when parallel with the witness of man and interwoven in it, the Holy Spirit gives His testimony to the power of Christ to save. We can observe two things: God's kingdom is being built not by might, nor by power, but by the Lord's Spirit. However, God does not build without us either. Just as a workman requires tools, so the Holy Spirit is in need of obedient instruments, of devoted lives, who may be used in His service and by whom Christ may be glorified (John 16: 14).

Whereas the first phase of the Spirit's work, when He is working for our conversion, occurs without our knowledge and will, His further work is not so. Now He requires conscious devotion and co-operation.

Throughout the world there are many people rejoicing over the forgiveness of their sins through the blood of Jesus Christ. Many people cherish the hope of a radiant and bright heaven, but they do not care for the salvation of others. Why is this? Is it because we do not teach clearly enough and stress that God is also looking for instruments today? Often we seemingly fail to educate members of our churches that after their conversion they should dedicate themselves to obedient service. He who saved them through the testimony of others wants to save others by them now. Be a witness for Christ. Let the Holy Spirit work through you to bring others to Christ. It is your duty as a Christian.

Are you God's children? Oh, then you who have been redeemed by His precious blood, do not restrain the Holy Spirit living in you and wanting to work by you (1 Thess. 5: 19)! Let Him have His way and complete His glorious work for, in, and through you.

111

Janos Hanyik

*The Reverend Janos Hanyik was born in Miske,
Hungary on June 20, 1923. After graduating from the
Baptist Theological Seminary in Budapest, he served as
a pastor in several Baptist churches: Pestujhely,
Ersekcsanad, Janoshalma, Kisköros and Bekes. He served
as the President of the Duna-Tisza-Közi Baptist
Association and as a member of the Baptist Theological
Seminary Council in Budapest. He is at present serving
as the pastor of the Baptist Church in Bekes.*

The other village

Janos Hanyik

Luke 9: 51–56

*When the days drew near for him to be received up,
he set his face to go to Jerusalem. And he sent
messengers ahead of him, who went and entered a
village of the Samaritans, to make ready for him;
but the people would not receive him, because his
face was set toward Jerusalem. And when his
disciples James and John saw it, they said, "Lord, do
you want us to bid fire come down from heaven and
consume them?" But he turned and rebuked them.
And they went on to another village.*

From the interesting verses of Scripture recorded by Luke concerning our Lord's journey toward Jerusalem we read about two
villages. In the first community Jesus was not received. In this
Samaritan village the people rejected the Lord outright because
it was plain that He was going to Jerusalem, to the Passover feast.
This attitude grew out of the hatred of the Samaritans towards
the Jewish people. But the Jews were no different; to them the
Samaritans were "dogs". There was a terrible antipathy between
the two nations. This explains why the Hebrews crossed the
Jordan and made a long detour when they came from the north
to Jerusalem. They absolutely refused to set their feet on
Samaritan soil. But Jesus did not make the traditional detour.
He went on a straight, determined course to the Holy City —
directly through Samaria.

Thus to the Samaritans He went, and since then straight to
the hearts of millions; just as He came to me at the age of twelve.
And He would come directly to you also; you who would listen to
the glorious gospel of the Lord Jesus Christ.

The Disciples React

Now the disciples reacted very negatively to the Samaritan rejection of their Lord. They wanted to call down fire from heaven to destroy those who would not receive Him. This is hardly "Christian", yet their attitude is somewhat understandable. In such a situation we would probably be tempted to jump into the affair and shout, "Jesus, don't let yourself be maligned. Reveal your identity! Defend your prestige! The man to whom was given all power over earth and heaven must not bear such insults! Call the fire down!" Of course, we are usually concerned about our own prestige also – perhaps even more so. Therefore we are ready to bring fire to this "wicked world"! I suppose if such circumstances depended on us, the world would have been destroyed many times over. We would probably have called fire down on each other so often that all would be consumed. Such is the nature of our own sinfulness in protecting our self-image and prestige. But Jesus did not react in such a manner to the situation. He simply went on to another village instead of raising dispute or pronouncing judgment.

What do you think was the motivation of our Lord in departing from this Samaritan village? Was it a withdrawal or retreat? Was it a resignation to defeat? Or could it be a triumphal march? Yes, it was a triumph – a triumph of mercy and grace.

Now whom do you identify with? Do you find yourself identifying with the threatening disciples or with the quiet Jesus? Christians, we must follow the Lord Jesus! Believe that the truly strong is not the one who shouts for vengeance or takes retribution in his own hands. Rather, it is he who offers his other cheek. That is victory. Hate never changes people. Jesus does not need force, inquisition, crusades, nor Christians bearing arms to further His Word.

Some Lessons to Learn

But now let us journey on to the other village with the disciples (v. 55b). And as we leisurely travel, let us reflect on the situation that occurred. We can learn many challenging things from the Lord Jesus and how He dealt with the Samaritan reactions. First, we learn that the Son of Man did not come to destroy men's lives, but to save them. God gave a *Saviour* to this world, not a destroyer. God is Love and He loved the world so much that He gave His only Son. If God loves us so much, so we must in turn relate to people with the same quality of love. We must not meet people with judgment, but with a merciful and gracious heart. And this kind of love is anything but weakness, cowardice or withdrawal. It is progress and victory.

Secondly, we discover from the event that God shows no partiality. Every nation and every people are of supreme value in His eyes, even if they belong to other races or religions. Jesus' teaching is in opposition to any kind of prejudice; religious, national, racial or what have you. God loves the Samaritans as well as the "chosen people". Jesus never solves problems shallowly – but radically. And He settled the question of the Samaritan-Jewish hatred. How? On the basis of love! Looking at the Samaritans' origin, history, problems, injuries and their relationship to the Hebrews and the Romans, He accepted them as they were. He knew the reasons that made the people such as they were. He knew that these people were a rejected people. But He also knew that love would be able to change them. The account of the Samaritan woman, the thankful Samaritan leper whom Jesus cured and the parable of the Good Samaritan show how He related in love to these despised people. Jesus always effected change in people's hearts through love, understanding and compassion.

And we too must turn to those from whom others turn away. Many people are suspicious and antagonistic because nobody trusts in them. Some are aggressive because they were always crushed down and never had love shown to them. Believe that love will change them. Love them – relate in depth to them. You will be acting as Jesus; you will be changed and they will change also.

The Blessings Follow

Finally, we should look at the blessings that result from following Christ all the way. For the disciples in our Scripture passage, it meant going on to another village. Of course, we do not always understand God's way: "My thoughts are not yours, neither are your ways my ways." But much blessing came from the fact that Jesus went to another village. As the group moved on to the next community, ten lepers waited for Jesus, and He miraculously healed them. How good it is that Jesus chose this way. Moreover, here were waiting for Him a sick woman as well as a blind man. These, too, Jesus healed. What a blessed experience it must have been for the disciples to witness these events.

Then look forward a moment and think of the evangelist Philip who went to the city of Samaria to preach Christ to the people there. The crowds with one accord gave attention to what Philip said. Perhaps the Samaritans recalled these very events and were thus open to Philip's message. The love of Jesus was the starting-point of the awakening in Samaria. If Jesus had called fire on them, Philip could never have called down the fire of the Holy Spirit on them. What a difference between the fire the early disciples wanted to call down and that which later fell because of Philip's ministry!

In closing, let me remind you of the apostle John who had been the "son of thunder". Through love he became Jesus' "beloved disciple". This lesson must have been a tremendous one for John. It changed his whole attitude and his entire character. He learned the essential lesson of love and suffering for others in Jesus' name.

How wonderful were the blessings and results because Jesus went this way. Come let us go with Jesus into the next village! Amen!

Sermons from
POLAND

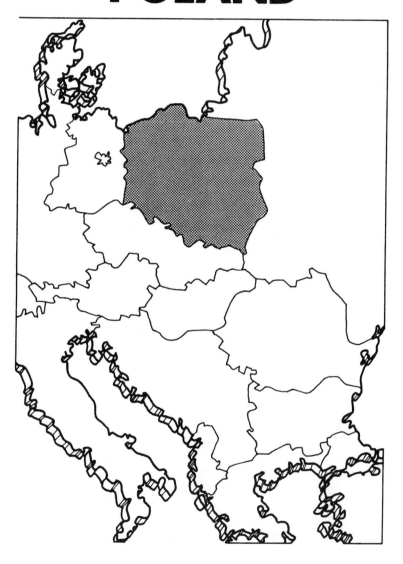

Michael Stankiewicz

The Reverend Michael Stankiewicz, a Baptist pastor in Poland, has faithfully served Christ for many years in his country. He has taken a leading role in his denomination, holding important offices. He is at present the pastor of a Baptist church in Warsaw.

In the face of guilt and love

Michael Stankiewicz

Genesis 3: 9–11

But the Lord God called to the man, and said to him, "Where are you?" And he said, "I heard the sound of thee in the garden, and I was afraid, because I was naked; and I hid myself." He said, "Who told you that you were naked? Have you eaten of the tree of which I commanded you not to eat?"

It was in a little town. The trial was under way. The young man was seated in the defendant's chair. The mother, seated in the first row among the people, wept bitterly; her only son was being judged. She had never thought the day would come when she would see him there. She had dreamed about a magnificent future for her boy. She wanted him to become a famous man. But, now look at what had become of him; he was a common criminal. And he was judged guilty. He was tried by the law and found guilty of the crimes of which he was accused. All the dreams and hopes of the loving mother were dashed to the ground. After the judicial sentence, the mother went up to her son and despite her bitter disappointment, stretched out her hands, drew her son close, kissed him, and said among her tears: "When are you going to return to your mother's home?" How marvellous is the depth of a mother's love.

Adam's Sin was Judged

This sad picture reminds us of the third chapter of Genesis. It reminds us of our forefather Adam, who also found love in the face of guilt. Let me direct your mind toward this sad, yet joyous picture.

At one time our planet earth was clothed with darkness and chaos. Then the Creator made order in our universe. And God saw that it was all good, because it descended from His own self, the mighty Creator. He then made man, the crown of creation. Man alone in this whole world bears resemblance to God, for man was made to have fellowship with God.

Temptation Comes to Man

The first man, therefore, enjoyed fullness of life, moral self-knowledge and self-consciousness. It was a very good period in the life of man. But then temptation struck. Somehow the snake became a sensible being and could speak. His tempting words promised to our first parents equality with God through usurping power for themselves for the setting of standards of moral good and moral evil. But this was the "big lie", and man, deluded by Satan, fell.

Thus evil invaded the human family. The wings of the soul of the first man were broken. And now, we all must agree that evil is surely in the world. Every age and every person manifests evil and as a consequence every one of us stands guilty before God; just as did Adam and Eve.

Look at the past; at history, literature, philosophy! The Middle Ages strongly emphasized the guilt of man. But then humanism tried to create a free man. The enlightenment came with its atheism and attempted to give man the verdict "not guilty". But romanticism again showed the guilt of man in attempting to wrestle with the problem of guilt and punishment. Then naturalism came on the scene and minimized the morality of man and gave him an image of equality with nature. But on the heels of naturalism came existentialism to remind man of his perplexity, fear and awe in the face of a meaningless life.

Guilt Is Unavoidable

History presents many different views of man and of his developing thought through the ages. But the truth is that man is always faced with guilt. The Bible presents the image of guilty men at the very inception of life, and literature demonstrates the guilt of man through the ages. And surely we are not free from this in our time. Contemporary ideologies have not found the answer.

Look around us! Granted, there is much good in the heart of man. But also, there is much that is evil. Of course, the evil in our day has a very civilized, cultured character: it is mixed with good, making it difficult to differentiate the one from the other. But it is still very real. And we are as guilty as our forefathers; guilt lies at the very foundation of our life.

I do not want to dwell on the dark side of our contemporary experience. But we must realize how deceived many people are today concerning the reality of sin. People are always saying that sin does not exist. But if they are right, why are there so many broken homes? Why are there so many complaints and so much hate in the world? Why is there so much weeping and suffering? Why, I ask you, why? Think a moment! Why, and again I ask, why?

The answer is quite simple and elementary: nothing has really changed since the time of Adam. Evil has only taken a new form. It is still the same and still separates us from God and complicates our lives. Sin, separating us from our Maker, causes us to lose fellowship with God and thus life becomes empty and meaningless. Somehow we all feel this. We implicitly know we need help. We seem to know that we are in a most difficult situation. Is there any way out?

The Answer

Yes, thank God, there is an answer. Our guilt and sin can experience forgiveness; sadness can be turned into joy; despair gives way to calm; doubt turns into certainty; darkness changes to light. And that wonderful forgiveness, joy, calm, certainty and light centre in the love of God.

God Comes to the Rescue

Dear brethren, the Bible tells us that God has come to the rescue of man. God sought out Adam. God called to him, "Where are you?" (Gen. 3:9). How much this question speaks of sympathy

124

and love! Thus we can now say with certainty that God deeply cares for the misfortune of man. God does not leave man alone in his difficult situation. We have all experienced how helpful it is when somebody stands beside us and talks with us when we need help. God did just that for Adam.

In one sense, however, the conversation between God and man came to a sad end: "God sent man forth from the garden of Eden to till the ground from which he was taken" (Gen. 3: 23). Listen carefully to the last words: "the ground from which he was taken". It was a logical consequence of disobedience. But there is also a marvellously bright note in the dialogue between God and Adam. The Bible tells us clearly that God does not leave man forever alone. God found a way of salvation for man. Therefore, although there was a righteous punishment, there was also love; God's great love for His erring creation.

The conversation of God with man also convinces us that love comes to the world to lift man from his fall. Guilt had separated man from God. Adam tried to hide among the trees, but love sought him out. God wanted to have fellowship with him. And love covered his spiritual nakedness. Guilt destroyed; love built. Guilt ruined; love drew him out of ruin.

Thus the struggle between God and evil began – between God and Satan. This warfare of Satan with mankind implies that a real blow for Satan will be struck! "I will put enmity between your seed and her seed; he shall bruise your head, and you shall bruise his heel" (Gen. 3: 15). And in this bruising strike, we see the final and ultimate defeat of evil and Satan's hosts. This is a prophecy of Good News. This is the victory of God's love in Jesus Christ. The Cross had to be! It was God's way of salvation. And God's love is best expressed in the Cross of our Lord and Saviour Jesus Christ.

Socrates said, "If you cannot be a good man, you should kill yourself." But God's love turned this around; He laid down His life for us, because God in Jesus Christ sacrificed Himself to save man. "For God so loved the world that he gave his only Son" (John 3: 16). A leader of a state may kill millions for his own glory. But our spiritual Leader, God in Jesus Christ, gave Himself to save millions of people. This is a different principle entirely. Do you see it?

125

Man Alone Is Helpless

The symbol of the flaming sword, the symbol which ends the story of man's guilt, shows the absolute impossibility of man's return to paradise by his own power. Therefore, we must emphasize and constantly repeat that between heaven and earth stands the Cross. This is the way into God's love, and that alone which lifts man from his sin and guilt.

Dear brethren, let me quietly ask you: "What do you think about your own guilt and the power of God's love?" Listen to the Bible, hear what it says! The Scriptures state, "For there is no distinction; since all have sinned and fall short of the glory of God, they are justified by his grace as a gift, through the redemption which is in Christ Jesus" (Rom. 3: 22–24). Further, the apostle Paul in personal desperation says: "Wretched man that I am! Who will deliver me from this body of death? Thanks be to God through Jesus Christ our Lord!" (Rom. 7: 24–25). David says a similar thing: ". . . my sin is ever before me. Against thee, thee only, have I sinned, and done that which is evil in thy sight, so that thou art justified in thy sentence and blameless in thy judgment. Behold, I was brought forth in iniquity, and in sin did my mother conceive me" (Ps. 51: 3–5).

The Word of God Speaks

The Bible gives us many such examples and states that we are all sinners. You can deceive yourself that this is not so, but if you examine yourself carefully, you will be convinced that the Bible is right. The Bible does not judge you, the Bible only states that you need justification; that you need inward harmony in your life, and above all, you need God. Moreover, the Bible convinces you that this is possible only through Jesus Christ. The Bible is intended to help you find new life in Christ.

You can reject the Bible, the Cross and God's justification. And you can attempt to justify such an action by saying: "I am a thinking man!" However, thinking man, can you learn from history? Remember Julian the Apostate who wanted to destroy Christianity in the fourth century. After the battle, when he was wounded and death was imminent, he dampened his finger in his own blood, lifted up his hand, and said: "Thou hast conquered, O Galilean." And somehow or other he found the love of

God overcoming his sin and guilt as he yielded to Christ.

Or remember Renan who wrote much about Christ. He had rejected the Son of God throughout his life. But as he lay on his death bed he said: *"Gekreuzigter!"* He found himself face to face with his guilt, but he called on God and found peace.

And do not forget the thief on the cross. His whole life was devoted to evil. He hung there beside Jesus. He was in the grip of guilt, but he too called on God's love, and he found inward peace and the certainty of salvation.

No, the Bible does not judge you. The Bible wants to help you. The Bible says that God has a place for you in His kingdom and faith is the way to enter that kingdom. You can experience justification by faith in Jesus Christ because of what He did on the Cross. Then, your guilt is removed. You find yourself, not in the grip of guilt, but in the grip of God's love, just as your forefather Adam. Oh, come out from behind the trees of sin, look on the Cross. This is where God's love is to be found.

A comparison can be made here. The Old Testament presents the picture of the fall of man. The New Testament shows the picture of the salvation of man. We can see the close connections between these images, e.g. Eve–Mary; Adam–mankind; Adam among the trees – Jesus Christ on the tree of the Cross; the blood of the animals for covering the sin of man – the death of God's Son for the washing away of the sins of all mankind. God's love is always the same. The world may change, but the Cross stands steadfast forever as the supreme manifestation of the love of God for sinful mankind.

Dear friend, God loves you. God is deeply concerned about you. His love wants to lift you to the dignity of a son. His love can cleanse all your sins. Do you know that the blissful experience of forgiveness is for you? You can take it by faith, if you will.

Love Can Conquer

Guilt leads to death; love leads to life. But love seeks mutuality. Love cannot exist without mutuality. If God loves you, you should love God in return. The issue is, therefore, do you love Christ? I do not mean to love His teaching, or some dogmas, forms, gifts, or even your salvation. But do you love Jesus Christ Himself? That is the real issue. Do you love Him personally, consciously and surely? This question concerns the essence of your Christianity and the answer to this question proves the power and quality of your faith. Your love should be alive and active.

Do you remember Peter, faced with guilt after the resurrection? Jesus asked, "Do you love me?" Peter loved and he lived. You can make the same decision; love and live!

Dear brethren, most of us have lived many years and have made many mistakes. But do not worry about the past; think about the future. You can find love and forgiveness in the face of guilt by trusting Christ and then the future will be new and glorious.

Remember that God suffers because of your sin. The content of the Cross says this and life affirms this. Oh, how God wants to meet you. Remember that though we have fallen, Christ can rescue us. Jesus Christ stands waiting for you. He gently asks: COME BACK HOME! Come to him now!

The re-creation of the individual

Michael Stankiewicz

2 Corinthians 5: 17

Therefore, if anyone is in Christ, he is a new creation; the old has passed away, behold, the new has come.

I once attended an art exhibition. Among the many paintings I saw I remember one especially; it made an unusual impact on my mind. It was the picture of a globe on which a man stood with the Bible in his hand. Various ideas and concepts whirled around him. Several hands stretched out from the globe and reached up to the man with the Bible. And every outstretched hand shouted the words, "Here is a new idea for you!"

The artist seemingly wanted to show the great interest and curiosity of man in gaining insight into truth and reality. He also attempted to picture the difficulties of the Christian believer in our contemporary society. Ideas constantly assail the believer. At times he is tempted to ask: "What should I choose? Where should I stand? How should I live? What is truth? Where shall I find the answer to the meaning of life?" Of course, these are the ultimate questions, and for these queries, we must find an answer.

The Bible tells us that God created man "in his own image". Moreover, God invited man into fellowship with Himself and gave man jurisdiction over all the world. Man thus became the most important of all creation. Man enjoys a unique position in God's economy. It is quite natural, therefore, that an all-pervading curiosity should exist in man. Further, history teaches us that this innate curiosity and seeking of ideas has not really changed throughout the ages. Look at the progress of human history!

Is There an Answer?

The ancient world had its religions, its laws, its philosophy and ethics. Even though the ancient cultures gave to the world many stable concepts, ideas which live today, they did not give absolute certainty to their people. Try as they might, the real meaning of life eluded them. Did anyone have a truly satisfying answer? Yes, the apostle Paul did! And he presented something entirely new; something fascinating, something that had the ring of authenticity.

Of course, this "something new" was not new. Many ancient cities, including Corinth, had many interesting people who proclaimed new ideas, new cults, and sought new ways to quench spiritual thirst. Yet, the apostle Paul could say that his message is the *only* one that could meet man's deepest need. And many believed him and new churches were formed.

But Paul was not naive about the situation. It is quite clear that he knew very well the ferment of the ancient world. He recognized that the local churches would have their problems with pagan philosophies. He knew these congregations well; he had established many of them. Thus he felt a deep concern for them. This is why he emphasized in his letters that the "inner man" must be constantly renewed. He recognized that continual renewal of strength in Christ was vital if the churches and the believers who made them up were to survive. And this strength came as the apostle states it: "in Christ". The whole meaning of spiritual life centres in Paul's great concept, "in Christ", i.e., being united with Jesus Christ in a similar fashion as He is united with the Father, for that is the real meaning of the idea. Now does this approach have any meaning for our *practical* life? Is it not too mystical? Moreover, what does this concept mean for us today?

History's Answers

Before we attempt an answer, we must turn again to history. Even after the fall of many ancient ideologies, the following generations seemed to profit little, for they went the same basic way. Although each new culture proclaimed something "new" for man, it was essentially a revamping of the same old ideas.

For example, the humanism of the later Middle Ages destroyed the principles that had held sway for some time. It maintained that these principles were irrelevant to current issues. It proclaimed a "new man", "new ethics", and "new principles" of life. It represented all things "new". Humanism gained the ascendancy and put to death the scholasticism of the Middle Ages. But then, the Baroque period did the same thing to humanism; and the Enlightenment replaced the Baroque; Romanticism phased out the Enlightenment; Positivism eliminated Romanticism; Naturalism superceded Positivism; and Modernism slew Naturalism.

Similarly, history reveals the same thing for many other intellectual disciplines such as philosophy, music, the arts or medicine. Of course, we cannot ignore these past attainments of human thinking. They do provide experience and they did sincerely seek a way to the truth. The quest itself was not evil.

And what about today as we turn to view our contemporary life? What do we see? First of all, we see an affluence the world has never known before. We also see tremendous development in knowledge, economics, sociology, medicine, literature, music and painting. Contemporary man has covered the expanses of the earth – even space. He has discovered many laws of life and has delved into many secrets of nature. Therefore we often hear these kinds of phrases: "new world", "new life", "new human strength". And this is not all!

The literary world constantly gives us new novels, dramas, comedies. Pedagogy presents new educational methods. Science puts forth new concepts and theories. Art fosters new forms; music, new composition. The shops all bulge with new clothes, shoes, refrigerators, vacuum cleaners, cars and new packaging of food. We build new buildings with near perfect architecture. We receive new philosophical and sociological views; even new theological theories and a thousand other "new" things. Of course, this is all very well because life must go forward. There is a certain value in development.

But can we face reality honestly for a moment? Do these outward signs of progress really change our life in any ultimate sense? All these things, these *new* things, they endure only a very short time. They soon become old as something else comes along to replace them; and life seems much the same as far as any ultimate principle is concerned.

Then, can we face a second truth? Did these outward signs of progress bring us any lasting happiness? People today seem a shipwrecked people, a disappointed people, a people who have faith only in man, in mere human ideals, in that which our new humanistic civilization created. And the result? Look at the record! How can we explain the horrors of the last world war? How can we explain the assassination of President John Kennedy, of Martin Luther King and many others? How can we understand people who burn themselves as a sign of protest over political events? How can we explain the fact that people live such isolated lives? How can we explain the fact that there is so much evil, so many wrecked lives?

We can create new philosophical, sociological and theological views. We can call these movements by great names. But the truth remains, the "new" is so often nothing but the humanistic "old".

Is there a way out of this situation? We cannot stop our lives. Nor can we cross out the events of our contemporary life. We cannot reject people; we cannot ignore human suffering. We must *help now*. And this is what Christianity is all about. Faith in Christ has an eternal dimension to be sure, but we must live on earth in the meantime. And we are on earth, as God's people, *to serve*.

Therefore, Christians must reach out to others in need. We should deny ourselves, meet needs, help create the conditions for the acceptance of Christ, and trust God to bring about the renewal of individual life. Christianity is not a crystalized concept, but a constant renewal of life "in Christ".

Nicodemus Finds some Answers

Let me illustrate this principle through an event which took place in the time of Jesus Christ. And though it took place 2000 years ago, it is very relevant to our contemporary life. Remember the story of Nicodemus? One night Nicodemus came to Jesus and spoke with Him about individual re-creation. The dialogue that ensued presents the picture of a seeking soul and the Saviour.

Nicodemus had just about everything, at least as far as the standards of that day were concerned. Nicodemus had a very high social position. He was educated. And he was quite religious. Still, he had deep-seated problems. But he had heard about Jesus Christ. He had heard of His teachings and miracles. So he came to Christ with his doubts and spiritual poverty. You see, he had serious questions at the very depth of his soul: How could the Kingdom of God be seen, and how could he enter it? What did the Kingdom even mean? He wanted to have spiritual beauty, truth, goodness, peace, joy and godliness. But where were the answers to be found?

Jesus Christ gave him a clear, concrete, decisive answer: "You must be born again." He had to experience a full, inward transformation. The natural man is dead and far from God. Therefore, Christ told him a simple truth: No one can enter the Kingdom of God unless he is born of water and the Spirit (John 3: 5).

Cannot enter the Kingdom! Strong words to be sure! Yet, these are the words of Christ. Man simply cannot be right with God by himself. We must be born again by the power of the mighty Son of God. And to be "born again" means "the old has gone, the new has come" (2 Cor. 5: 17). Life can begin anew.

In the marvellous experience of rebirth and renewal we find two sides: the negative – cleansing of the old nature by repentance, and the positive – recreation of the Spirit to new life by faith in Christ.

You may say that it is difficult to understand this process. True, but there are many processes we do not understand. We can take two very simple examples. We put our dirty clothes in the water, add the soap and do not think further about the process of cleaning. The chemist can explain this process, but few of us even think about it. We just do it. Or take the process of nature. The rose grows in the soil. We know that it draws sustenance from the earth, transforms it, and lifts it up in the beauty of the blossom. Not many understand the process, but we see the beauty and we enjoy it. There are a multitude of things we utilize that we do not understand.

Now Nicodemus just could not understand what it meant to

be born anew. He did not seem to be able to grasp what Jesus was talking about. However, after the death of Christ, the entire picture changed. After the tremendous events of the Passion he apparently saw in Jesus Christ the Saviour. I say this because we read that "Nicodemus also, who had at first come to him by night, came bringing a mixture of myrrh and aloes, about a hundred pound's weight" (John 19: 39). Nicodemus went to the tomb; he identified himself with Christ openly.

The night conversation had now apparently become clear. He had to act upon Jesus' words, even if he did not fully comprehend all the truth. And he seemingly came through with a genuine commitment. When even the disciples left their Master, when the whole world condemned Jesus, Nicodemus was willing to be identified with the Christ of the cross. He must have been "born again" and experienced "the old gone, the new come".

Jesus Satisfies the Soul's Needs

Let me earnestly ask you: What is the state of your soul? I ask you this not to judge you, but because of my love for you. D. T. Niles said that the evangelist is no more than "One beggar telling another beggar where to find bread." I am a beggar, you are a beggar too. I am a sinner, you are a sinner too. Before God we are spiritual beggars, so we should seek spiritual food. Our predicament is the same. We should help one another. I simply want to help you to Christ, the "Bread of Life".

The apostle Paul said that Jesus Christ "has delivered us from the dominion of darkness and transferred us to the Kingdom . . ." "Delivered" and "transferred"! These two are very expressive terms. They imply that the nature of man is closely tied with darkness, and that we need the power of God to tear us away from this darkness. If you uproot a plant, you remove it from the ground. If you want to tear yourself out of darkness, you must be willing to experience a real uprooting. But the new "ground" to which you are "transferred" is tremendous – it is "in Christ".

Perhaps you ask: "When will the new nature come? How does it come?" I can answer your questions this way. First of all, you must find Christ. And if you want to find Christ, you must acknowledge your sins. If you say you have no sins, there is no hope. You will never find Jesus unless you are willing to confess your sin and need of a Saviour. But if you will say, "God, I am a sinner, I need your help, your love, your understanding," then God will be merciful to you.

The First Step

This first step is not easy. To acknowledge this truth is painful. To kill my self-esteem; to destroy my self-complacency, self-conceit, self-confidence, self-delusion, self-dependence; in other words, to destroy the outward shell of self, is extremely difficult. What will people say? What will people think? But you should do as Mary Magdalene – fall down at Christ's feet and give the best of your life. You must throw yourself at Christ's feet as an "alabaster jar of very expensive ointment". Yes, Christianity is costly! But Jesus Christ gave His life for you and that was *infinitely* costly.

Now this "destruction" of the self leads to a radical out-and-out change in one's whole character and nature. All the negative aspects of your life change to positive ones. You will think in new patterns which you receive from God. If you hated, you will love. If you had secret sins, you will drop them.

A story may help to explain this principle. Once a recluse lived with his dog near a large city. He was very evil and so was his dog. Both understood each other. On one occasion, however, the recluse went to a revival meeting. He saw himself for the first time as he really was. He deeply repented. He was converted. So radical was the change that his face even changed. He came back home. The dog jumped at him and bit him.

One very profound fact lies at the bottom of this rather humorous story, however; evil hates the truth. Everybody recognized the recluse as a changed man, even his dog.

When you live out your experience of Christ, people, things, surroundings – everything – becomes different because God's love dwells in your heart. Life takes on new meaning because your inner life is changed. Your mind slowly, but systematically, undergoes a beautiful process of renewal. This leads to a transformation of your entire nature. You learn not only to love people, but you will begin to ask, how can the world be changed; how can needs be met? The old selfish way of life has gone, the completely new, selfless way of life has come.

Above all, you value heavenly things. The things of Christ take their proper place in your experience. These things become the measure of your goals in life. Your earthly existence comes into contact with real life; eternal life.

Similarly, your spirit is lifted up to new heights, and full spiritual transformation is effected. True religion is a matter of a vital relationship with God. It is not primarily a matter of ethics or moral striving. Nicodemus had to learn that. He thought that wisdom could work out the rules of conduct. The rabbis taught that all one needs to do is to observe the Law in every detail. This, as they said it, would lead to salvation. But as Nicodemus found out, one's relationship with God depends wholly on faith in the gracious work of Christ. This sets one free from legalism and formal sacramentalism.

I do not mean to say that we are to withdraw from this earthly life. Never! Earthly life is a gift from God. You should not cross out your temporal life. God gives the whole world to enjoy. But you should relate your entire temporal life to God through Jesus Christ. This is what the new birth effects through the mystery of redemption. The old has gone, the new has come. If you have constant contact with God, you will always receive His divine spiritual energy for your temporal life.

The Permanence of New Life

Is individual re-creation a once-for-all act? Yes! Your meeting with Christ, your acceptance of Christ, the understanding of yourself and your radical out-and-out willingness to let your entire nature be renewed by God is surely a single, once-for-all, act. But at the same time, it is just the beginning. You were born again, but you must grow. You must mature into the likeness of God – in whom all is new.

And there is a finality about the new birth. The apostle John said: "I saw a new heaven and a new earth; for the first heaven and the first earth had passed away, and the sea was no more" (Rev. 21: 1). The goal is to share in the new heaven and the new earth. But, until that day, you are on the earth. Therefore, God wants to make you useful for service.

The apostle Paul told the members of the church at Corinth: "If any one is in Christ, he is a new creation." This means that Christianity is a *constant process* of the renewal of our nature. This is most important. Because you are in Christ, you must experience a *constant* renewal of your nature. Christianity is not just a *single* act of acceptance of Christ, baptism, and other practices. No! Christianity is the *constant* act of the renewal of our nature.

Also, Christianity is the constant process of *perfecting*. It is true that you started with all things new, but you will be plagued constantly by the old nature in your daily life. It will attack you! You must fight – as Christ in Gethsemane said: "My soul is very sorrowful . . . if this cannot pass unless I drink it, thy will be done". "Watch and pray that you may not enter into temptation; the spirit indeed is willing, but the flesh is weak". So, you must fight the old nature of the flesh.

But you can choose that which leads you and brings you nearer to God. You have freedom in Christ. Therefore, you should choose that which is spiritually helpful to you. Life will always bring new problems. We will be constantly assailed by new events and circumstances. But you can choose that which will enrich your soul, that which will bring you nearer to God, that which will perfect your selfhood, that which will help you to mature in Christ. Your personal spiritual experience will then be a constant process of perfecting.

An old folk story of our country Poland relates that once in a small village a daughter left her elderly mother. The daughter wanted to see the world. So she left her mother all alone. Sin robbed her of all that was great, noble, and sublime. She finally decided to come back to her mother's home. She resolved to return during the night so that people would not see her.

When she arrived at the little hamlet and made her way to the old house, she pressed the door handle. The door opened. She entered. The mother woke up and said: "My daughter, my door was always open. Since you left my home, the door has remained unlocked. I knew that you would come back to me. I love you. I shall help you. Welcome home, dear one! "

In a similar fashion, the door of the Kingdom is always open. Jesus Christ is always waiting for you. Sin destroys. It robs you of that which is great, noble and sublime. But come to God with your doubts, your troubles, your sins and ask Him for His forgiveness and re-creating power; ask Him to take away the old and to bring the new through Jesus Christ our Lord. Decide now! Life and death hang in the balance.

137

Sermons from
YUGOSLAVIA

Josip Horak

Dr Josip Horak was born in Derventa, Bosnia,
Yugoslavia. His father came from Czechoslovakia and
his mother, of Czech origin, was a native Yugoslav. His
father was a businessman and lay Baptist pastor first in
Yugoslavia and later in Czechoslovakia. It was there
he died a few years ago.

Dr Horak graduated in law with a LL.B. degree from
Belgrade University in 1939, and received a Doctor of
Science degree in Economics in 1956 from Zagreb
University.

He has worked in the business world, serving in
different state companies as economic consultant and
financial director, until 1970. In 1972 he was elected as
Professor of Economics in the University of Zagreb.

He is a layman, active in the Baptist church for many
years. He served as the first president of the Baptist
Theological Seminary, then in Zagreb, from 1953
to 1957. In 1947 he was elected president of the Baptist
Union of Yugoslavia. He has been successively
re-elected every three years and serves as president at the
present time. He also serves as pastor of the Baptist
church in Zagreb. He is a well known and deeply
appreciated speaker on radio broadcasts to Yugoslavia,
seven times weekly, through Trans World Radio, Monte
Carlo and Bonaire (Netherland Antilles).

He was the organizer of the Billy Graham evangelistic
meetings in Zagreb (1967), and served as Dr. Graham's
interpreter. He is responsible for the remarkable written
account of that historic event: Euro 70.

The great discovery of a young man

Josip Horak

Luke 15: 17

But when he came to himself he said, "How many of my father's hired servants have bread enough and to spare, but I perish here with hunger!"

It has been said that the Luke 15 parable of the prodigal son is the most beautiful story ever written. And the reason is, the story is told by One who knows best the hearts of many prodigal sons and daughters.

This story is obviously very well known; so well known that many consider its message exhausted. Thus they hold that it is useless to speak any more on the subject. But this "gospel in miniature", as we can well describe the story, is so rich in spiritual truth that its indescribable richness can never be depleted. It is a story relevant for every man of every age. You see, we all find ourselves in some sense the prodigal son. This is why the parable Jesus told is so pertinent for today.

But though the theologians are most familiar with the parable, this is not true of all by any means. During evangelistic meetings in various parts of our country, we asked those present if they had ever heard the story about the prodigal son. Seldom did anyone answer positively. So, in our country at least, there are today many who need to hear it.

And even in those parts of the world where most have heard this story many times, it is possible that even some of those who have heard it have never made the great discovery that the young man in the story made. So it has a message for us all. Let us look at it closely.

142

Reading the text in Luke 15:17 we find these very significant words: *"And when he came to himself . . ."* After becoming absolutely destitute, it appears that it did not take long for this young man to make a most vital discovery. And what was that great discovery? The young man discovered what millions of people have yet to find, namely, the genuine meaning of life, the true meaning of personal freedom, and life's ultimate goal.

Now, where does one find this elusive meaning of life? Many seemingly spend their whole lives without comprehending it. Of course, many try to find it like the young man in this story; far from the Father! They wish to depart from Him as far as possible! (It is interesting that today's drug addicts also speak about their "trips".) Then, disillusioned with their lives in "the far country", that is, far from the Heavenly Father, they come to the conclusion that life is meaningless. It is no wonder that agnostic modern philosophers like Sartre teach that man's life is an exercise in futility. And today many have come to just such a conclusion. Yet, such an opinion is understandable, for people who refuse the new life Christ alone can give cannot find any meaning at all. It is impossible to experience the good life without the source of all good. Jesus Christ describes it in these words: "Without me you can do nothing." Simply put, life without Christ is "nothing".

Then there are those who try to find meaning for their lives – again like the prodigal son – in physical pleasure; in self-indulgence. But man was created "in the image of God", and for God. He was given life so that he may please his Creator. And if he does not, if he lives only for self-pleasure, in reality he pleases only the devil. He repeats what Adam did in the first act of disobedience to God. "He that is not with me is against me," said our Saviour. There can never be purpose and meaning in life when a man gives himself only to himself.

God created man to live a life which is worthy of man. This means living according to God's will and for His glory. This we must never forget; when a man does not uphold God's standard, the total degradation of human dignity inevitably results. So the prodigal son, when he had spent all (and it went quickly, because it is much easier to spend than to gain) had to accept the lowliest job for a Jew; to feed the "unclean" swine. But the worst was yet to come.

Pleasure Corrupts

People who search for meaning in pleasures, often finish in moral decay and perversity which can degrade them to the level of beasts – even below it at times. There is a saying which states that "the corruption of the best is the worst". We need not marvel then that many who reject God's morality, who do not want to accept the Creator for their Guide, sometimes commit deeds of which animals would be ashamed. But it was not God's plan in the original creation that man, this most perfect of God's creatures, should live such a degraded life as to be forced to feed on the husks the swine ate. How tragic it was that the prodigal son had to come to the very nadir of his existence before he could discover the true meaning of his life; to "come to himself".

But this young man had something more to discover. He had left his home searching for freedom outside the narrow confines of his parents' home, just as many young people do today – perhaps even more so than when our Lord first related it. How relevant the old parable is! The son in this story apparently thought that his father, and perhaps his older brother, were the cause of all his dissatisfaction. For this reason he happily left his home, coercing his father into giving him that to which, in some sense, he had no right at all. "Father, give me the portion of goods that falleth to me," insisted the young man. According to the then existing law, he could claim his estate only after the death of his father. But he did not want to wait; he wanted everything immediately. He didn't say: "Father, please, give me!" he simply commanded: "Father, *give* me!"

So he set out on his search for freedom like many a modern young man. But this anticipation of a new freedom proved an illusion, as it always does. Freedom is never found the way this young man sought it. What is "freedom" anyway? We recently read in our newspapers about the book of the American psychologist B. F. Skinner: *Beyond Freedom and Dignity*. The distinguished writer holds that it is the environment and not the inner being of the man which determines his behaviour. In connection

144

with this he draws an analogy with the behaviour of animals, which is determined by the complex influence of external factors in the environment. In other words, all of man's actions are determined solely by his environment and heredity. However, we must surely acknowledge that the behaviour of man is quite different from that of animals. This we believe because we hold that he is created "in the image of God". Thus man is essentially free. This is one of the basic truths that makes man a man.

But individual freedom must be responsible; it has to consider others if life is to be truly free. Our young man in the parable forgot this principle entirely. He disregarded the tears of his good father. Why should I consider others, he thought; all that is important is myself! Can such an attitude of individual freedom be right? Can that attitude bring meaning to life? Hardly!

In the book *Teaching Human Rights* of the United Nations there is a French text; "Leçons sur les Nations Unies et les institutions specialisées". It is issued by the French Ministry of National Education. In this interesting document we read; "Liberty consists in the power of doing whatever does not injure another. It is rooted in nature, its guiding principle is justice, its safeguard the law; its moral limit lies in this maxim: do not unto others what you would not that they do unto you."

Fortunately, the young prodigal learned the lesson, but he realized too late to save himself and others from grief. "When he came to himself", he saw that he had cruelly offended his father and that he had sinned terribly. But how wonderful it was that he saw the real issue, for he came to the place of decision and said, "I will arise and go to my father and will say unto him: 'Father, I have sinned against heaven and before thee . . . And am no more worthy to be called thy son . . .' "

A Great Discovery

Thus the young man discovered that true freedom includes responsibilities as well as rights, and that there is no right without duty. He became aware of his responsibility for his own deeds and he found that responsibility and duty must precede personal rights. Earlier he spoke, "Father, give me the portion of goods that falleth to me", and now, when he comes to himself, he speaks humbly, "Make me as one of thy hired servants." Now he speaks only about service! That is the beginning of true freedom. The essence of all genuine liberation is the willingness to be a "slave" to the rights of others.

Finally, our young man came to genuine self-discovery, "he came to himself". Earlier he attempted to run away from himself into a far country, to an alien atmosphere, but surprisingly he found himself there! He came to his spiritual maturity! For spiritual maturity is, in the final place, to find oneself. The ancient Greeks taught, "Know thyself! " The ancient Romans stated, "Control yourself! " But Christianity teaches that a man has to "*find* himself"! Our Saviour Jesus Christ said, "For what is a man profited, if he gain the whole world and lose himself, or be cast away?"

So the prodigal son came to the greatest of all discoveries. Through self discovery he found the way to the Father; back to God, back to life! But the way is not easy. One must recognize his own sin and failure. He must repent of that life of sin and go back to the Father. And this is far from easy. It takes a real man or woman to repent of one's sins and of a life lived without God.

I had a conversation with an outstanding communist once. He had been imprisoned because of his loyalties before the second world war. During the war he fought among the partisans. He said, "We now see that we cannot build a new society with old men. For a new society we need new men! " "It is true," I said to him. "There are only two things which are truly relevant today to make men new. But they were taught two thousand years ago by Jesus Christ. What are they? Repentance and the new birth." Of course, I then developed these ideas as I told him of Jesus Christ and His power to make men new – the kind of "newness" that is eternal and truly "free".

Now, what is repentance? What is this that is necessary if we are to find God (Luke 13: 3)? Well, earlier, the prodigal son tried to place the guilt for everything on those around him. That surely was not the answer. But when he had come to himself, he realized that the fault was basically *in himself*. He was in sin because of his departure from the father. And he not only recognized and regretted it intellectually, he *repented* of his actions. That is, "he arose, and came to his father . . ." He moved out of his far country. He turned with all of his heart

146

to the father. He presented himself to the father willing to be only a slave.

There are many who constantly regret their faults and sins, but never really repent. Thus, they always remain more or less the same. Jesus Christ is always willing to forgive sinners, but He asks something in return. He said on one occasion to a woman whose sins were forgiven, "Go, and sin no more." After the willingness to acknowledge one's sins, there must be sincere repentance and faith in Jesus Christ. Only then will the new birth take place. Only then will life be made new. Such was the experience of the prodigal son.

The Waiting Father

The gracious father waited with longing and patience for this moment. Every day he looked through the window expecting the return of his lost son. Here we see something quite remarkable; he never went to search for him and he never tried to over-persuade or coerce him to return home. The young man had to come to the knowledge that he had done wrong. He had to come to himself. He had refused to listen to his father's advice and he had to pay a heavy toll for his own stubbornness and disobedience. But it was just then that the young man made the greatest discovery of his life. He knew his father would receive him if he would only return home. What a discovery!

Sir James Simpson, the great Scottish scholar who discovered chloroform, once said that the greatest discovery of his life was not chloroform, but the fulfilment of his greatest need: Jesus Christ as his Saviour. It is my prayer that you, as a prodigal son, will also make this wonderful discovery. If you do, and will come to the Father through Jesus Christ, you too will find the marvellous reception only He can give. Come home now! The Father waits for you!

Franjo Klem

The Reverend Franjo Klem is at present serving as president of the Baptist Seminary in Novi Sad, Yugoslavia. His accomplishments are most unusual. After graduation from the Baptist Seminary in Budapest, Hungary, he served in both the German and Yugoslavian armies.

He has served as pastor of several churches in Yugoslavia and as an outstanding leader in his denomination. His present position takes him all over his country and outside his native Yugoslavia as well. No man is better known or loved by the churches than Franjo Klem. His insight, experiences and fearlessness in preaching the gospel of Christ are deeply moving and inspiring.

Maranatha

Franjo Klem

1 Corinthians 16: 22

If any one has no love for the Lord, let him be accursed. Maranatha.

The word *Maranatha* is of Aramaic origin. It came into use in the Greek language, the common language of the first century, and thus into usage in the New Testament. *Maranatha* means "the Lord is come", or "the Lord is coming", or "Lord, come!" The word was often employed as a greeting in apostolic times between the Christians. We greet each other today in Yugoslavia with *"Gospod s tobom* – God be with you", or *"Bog te blagoslovio* – God bless you". The word *maranatha* was used in a similar fashion between the early Christians. It became a sign of recognition between fellow believers.

It was to be expected that first-century Christians would take this word of greeting with all seriousness. These early believers held the second coming of Jesus Christ as one of the foundation stones upon which the Christian faith is built. Moreover, these Christians fully expected Jesus to return in their own day. This living hope thus motivated them to be vigilant and watchful. And this hope should move us today to be prepared and ready for Christ's glorious return.

Preparedness is Vital

The idea of preparedness is often found in the Scriptures. For example, on the night of the Israelite deliverance from Egypt, they *prepared* for the exodus by being dressed and girded with staffs in hand. In like manner, we as God's children today must be prepared for our ultimate deliverance, on the foundation of

150

Ephesians 6: 13–18: "girded with truth, and having put on the breastplate of righteousness and having shod your feet with the equipment of the gospel of peace; above all taking the shield of faith . . . the helmet of salvation and the sword of the Spirit." Our Lord is coming – and He is coming soon! *We must be prepared.*

There is a tremendous treasure and vast storehouse of Christian truth contained in the simple word *maranatha.* This is true because it centres on our Lord Jesus Christ. Of course, it implies initially His great act of self-giving when on the cross He cried out, "It is finished!" The great miracle of God's grace was manifest. After His triumphant resurrection, our Lord Jesus ascended into the heavens where He sits on the right hand of the heavenly Father and there intercedes for us. Concerning the great redemption act He thus accomplished, Jesus said of Himself, "I am the Alpha and the Omega, the first and the last . . . I died, and behold, I am alive for evermore, and I have the keys of death and Hades" (Rev. 1: 8, 18).

So, everyone who truly repents and believes in the Lord Jesus Christ and loves Him sincerely will be saved. This certainty of salvation is our living hope for victory and the ultimate perfection that awaits.

Jesus is Coming Again

But the word *maranatha* finds its essential meaning in the "deep yearning" all God's people experience for the second coming of Christ; as John cried out in Revelation 22: 20, "Yes, come Lord Jesus!" This is our "blessed hope" – and our fervent prayer.

However, we must also recognize a warning, an admonition, in the term. It is all very well to wish the Lord to come, but we must be prepared for that hour. John's prayer, "Yes, come Lord Jesus", can be sincerely uttered only if we are ready for that great meeting.

Dear friends, look at this principle from the perspective of a rather common occurrence. Let us say the telephone rings and you lift the receiver and ask, "Who is it?" Suddenly, you turn pale; your hands tremble; you find a chair to sit on. What is the reason for your fear and anxiety? Because over the telephone you heard the news you were totally unprepared to receive. We have all had experiences something like that. Life is filled with such occurrences.

Now let me ask, how would you react if our Lord were suddenly to return? Would you cry out, "O Lord, not yet! I am not prepared! Even though I am a Christian, not yet Lord; my love for you is so superficial and shallow. Not yet, Lord, I do not love my neighbour as I love myself; I do not even love my brothers and my sisters in Christ as they love me. Lord, don't come yet, I still cannot forgive those who have trespassed against me and who speak against me; I am still full of pride and conceit. Do not come yet, Lord, I have not cared enough for the 'flock' you gave me; nor have I used the talents that you gave me; I buried them for safe keeping. Do not come yet, Lord, my lamp has no oil; you'll find no fruit on my tree. Wait, Lord, a little longer, till I put my marriage in order, until I influence my children correctly, until I witness about you to my neighbours. Wait, because I want to sell my possessions and give the money to your cause and Kingdom. Don't come yet, Lord, I have unclean lips; I committed perjury against my brother and I spoke against my sister in Christ. Not yet, Lord, my heart is not clean. How can I meet you? No, Lord, no! I am backslidden in my Christian life. An ox knows his master and a donkey knows the crib of his master, but I do not know you . . . I left you. My head is sick and my heart is faint; from my head to my feet there is no soundness. I am pierced and bruised and wounded by festering sores; my wounds are not dressed or anointed with oil (Isa. 1). O Lord, not yet! " *Our Lord is coming – are you prepared?*

So the word *maranatha* has far more depth than just a friendly greeting or a sign of recognition between believers. It contains a serious warning and reminder of our great meeting with our Lord.

Are You Ready?

Oh, friend, my plea to you is, be prepared. Today, give yourself totally to your Lord, acknowledge your sins and spiritual coldness to Him. Repent, be reconciled, and your sins which were scarlet will be as white as snow (Is. 1: 18). Be prepared to meet your Lord. Be worthy of this great meeting, so that when you hear the glorious news, "I am coming soon," you will be able to say with joy, "Yes, come Lord Jesus! " MARANATHA!

152

When the crumbs become big loaves

Franjo Klem

John 6: 5–13

*Lifting up his eyes, then, and seeing that a
multitude was coming to him, Jesus said to Philip,
"How are we to buy bread, so that these people
may eat?" This he said to test him, for he himself
knew what he would do. Philip answered him,
"Two hundred denarii would not buy enough bread
for each of them to get a little." One of his
disciples, Andrew, Simon Peter's brother, said to
him, "There is a lad here who has five barley loaves
and two fish; but what are they among so many?"
Jesus said, "Make the people sit down." Now there
was much grass in the place; so the men sat down,
in number about five thousand. Jesus then took
the loaves, and when he had given thanks, he
distributed them to those who were seated; so also
the fish, as much as they wanted. And when they
had eaten their fill, he told his disciples, "Gather
up the fragments left over, that nothing may be
lost." So they gathered them up and filled twelve
baskets with fragments from the five barley loaves,
left by those who had eaten.*

During the public ministry of our Lord Jesus Christ, many
wonders and miracles took place. In performing these wonder-
works, Jesus had three aims in view. First, He did many of His
deeds because of men's need. Then, He performed miracles in

the attempt to help people see in Him the promised Messiah. Thirdly, with His wonders He edified His disciples. These are the principles that undergird the event recorded in our text.

It was for the third reason mentioned above that Jesus set His disciples a task; a really difficult task – actually, an impossible one. He asked, "How are we to provide bread, so that this people may eat?" Why did He ask this? Was the need of food so great that it was absolutely mandatory to do something? Hardly! I remember, when I was put into a concentration camp during the second world war, for several days we received nothing to eat. Yet, no one died of hunger. Jesus' question was not merely on the level of human need for food. The people would not have starved. The reason for putting this question to His disciples was quite different. The Scriptures state, "This he said to test them, for he himself knew what he would do." And truly, it was a probing test.

Now it must be made very clear that difficulties and testing times do not always come as God's punishment. Often they are a test of faith. God wants to see how His children will face their problems and sorrows. He wants to see how His followers will deal with their difficulties; how they will use their faith. Will they attempt to escape the issue because of the sorrow and trial of the problem; or will they exercise their faith and look to God to find a solution? Will they trust in their own ingenuity or will they trust in Him?

The Place of Testing

The genuine maturity of a Christian will become known not in a time when everything is going well, but in a time of testings and trials. This world of turmoil is the scene where God tests His servants. He puts them out as "sheep among the wolves", and it is only then that they taste the bitterness and sweetness of the words in Matthew 5: 11, where Jesus said, "Blessed are you when men revile you and persecute you and utter all kinds of evil against you falsely on my account." Of course, not all Christians must go through heavy tests, but every Christian, at one time or another, has to be tested in some way. He has to prove himself as a sound follower of Jesus Christ. Every man and woman who would follow Christ must take up his cross and follow his

154

Master and Saviour. Now, in our Scripture passage, Jesus is testing His disciples. He wants to see how they will deal with the problem of getting food for this multitude. Our text above demonstrates two human solutions to the quandary.

Solutions

First, there is Philip's solution. He answered Jesus' question by saying, "Two hundred denarii would not be enough bread for each of them to get a little." That is the way of human logic. A reasonable man of the world will logically look after the money, trying to figure out all the possibilities. Seemingly, Philip missed the whole point of Jesus' question. But we must not be too quick to judge Philip. After all, we in eastern Europe after the second world war faced the same situation. Most of our chapels needed repair. We did not have enough Bibles or hymnals. We faced a great lack of trained pastors, and money. Our resources were very meagre, and most important of all, we were experiencing a tremendous lack of freedom for missionary and evangelistic action in our country. We were just broken down. One day, while discussing our work and needs, someone of us said, "We can hardly do anything! We will have to wait for better times. We can do little until we will have more freedom, more money and opportunities." This was Philip's attitude and solution. Such a solution is natural and logical for a man who does not know the possibilities and power of our Lord Jesus. But such an attitude is wrong, for it lacks faith. Actually, Philip's faith was weak and short-sighted. And very often our faith is much akin to Philip's. But no solution to any problem will be found along these lines.

Then, secondly, there is Andrew's solution to the problem. He made a bit deeper attempt to meet the need than Philip. He discovered something of a resource. He found a lad with five barley loaves and two fishes. But he too confessed his helplessness, saying: "But what are they among so many?" Thus he also missed the real core of the issue at hand.

But at least we must credit Philip and Andrew with trying. When we are plagued with troubles and problems, the worst thing we can do is just do nothing. Weeping and wailing and complaining to the heavens and doing nothing solves nothing. We have to do all we can do. But more, we must then come praying to the

Lord. And, in principle, Andrew did this. He did what he could and then brought to Jesus what he did not have under his control. Our Lord does not expect from us impossible things, i.e., what we never shall be able to fulfill. Bearing His cross never means bringing us to an impasse. And I suppose it is doing what we can do in Christ's name that is ultimately of greatest value. It would be marvellous to preach the gospel to a great multitude like Billy Graham. But such great occasions probably will never come for most of us. Yet little things, opportunities for little deeds, can be found every day. It is a great error to cry for the great things and then trample over many little possibilities to glorify God. Jesus Himself said, "Well done . . . you have been faithful over a little, I will set you over much" (Matt. 25:21). So, what we have to do is to gather together our little money, our weak faith, our crippled freedom, all our crumbs, and give them into the hands of our Lord. And in doing this we are doing the most important thing, for we are mobilizing all our power and resources and funds; and although they are only little crumbs, when we give them to God, God's power will multiply them and wonders will happen.

God Has the Solution

Now let us see how Jesus met the problem for Philip and Andrew. Jesus did not accept Philip's mere human solution, nor did He find Andrew's solution the final answer. But an answer was forthcoming, for God does not know any "Stop". For Him everything is possible. Yet He needs us in His wonderful work. He wants us to be His collaborators. Thus he used Philip and Andrew in the solution of the problem, despite their weak and feeble faith. Therefore, with Him we can do great things. But we must recognize two important principles. First, we have to do what we can, although it will seem to us as little crumbs. Then, secondly, we need to surrender all to God and believe. And if our faith is no more than a grain of mustard seed, the crumbs will become big loaves. *That is God's solution!*

Sometimes the problems and sorrows seem to be just too heavy for us. But they are not too heavy for our God. When our power and our possibilities come to an end, there is God prepared to intervene with His creative power.

Today, in our country of Yugoslavia, we are enjoying not only a much greater freedom than in the past, but also the privilege of developing an organized mission work. Why, we could baptize thousands of new converts, build new church buildings, print books, and periodicals, and then do a multitude of meaningful things to God's glory. *And this we have done.* Thanks be to God for all His mercies.

But you ask, "How was it possible? How could you do this under your circumstances?" We have only one simple answer. We gathered our little crumbs, brought them to our Lord, and He blessed the little crumbs, and they became big loaves. These are the twelve baskets filled with blessings, which came back to us. Thanks be to God for His gracious mercy. And you can enjoy the same.

Sermons from
BULGARIA

Pastor Angeloff

Pastor Angeloff was a faithful minister of the gospel for many years in his native Bulgaria. Under difficult circumstances he held high the Banner of Christ. He was pastor of the Baptist Church in Sofia for some years.

He has just recently been called to his eternal reward. His sermon on heaven therefore has profound significance. What he preaches about he is now experiencing.

Longing for heaven

Pastor Angeloff

Philippians 1: 21

For me to live is Christ, and to die is gain.

We Christians often act like the unbelieving world. We preach that it is wonderful to be a Christian, to inherit heaven and be saved from hell! But when one of our dear ones is called home, we act as if all this were not true. Our conduct and deeds often imply that we must think this world is better than the next; that death is a tragedy. In our lack of faith we cry, Why? Why? Why, did this befall us?

We know that heaven is of infinite value, but so often after we have tasted all the pleasures of this world we put too much importance on the temporal. Yes, we agree that one must think about heaven, but often we seemingly feel its pricelessness only after old age comes, when health is gone and life becomes heavy to endure, when we are no more needed by anyone. We can develop the attitude that heaven is a place where one throws away the worn out and useless things; a kind of an old-age asylum which is better than nothing, but not half so good as this world.

Death and the Christian

But for the Christian death is never a tragedy. It should not be viewed as such. Actually, it is a glorious promotion. It is not a sad end, but a glorious beginning. People often say how sad that so and so died at such an early age! But this is a Satanic deceit. When a Christian dies, young or old, it is not sad, but glorious. As much as we feel the loss of our dear ones when they are gone, let us remember that our crying is selfish; in heaven there is only joy. No one from this "glorious land", if he could, would return to the mortal and decaying body which he left in order to finish the life he had planned to live on this earth.

True, as the Word of God tells us, death is a dreadful thing for the unrepenting sinner, but it is glorious for the child of God. Blessed and happy are the Christians who are dead in Christ (Rev. 14: 13). "For me to live is Christ, and to die is gain" (Phil. 1: 21).

According to the above-mentioned verses, the Christian should *long* for heaven. We know that the Lord Jesus Christ can come any moment and take away His Church. What a blessed experience for the true believer! But if He does not come now and delays His return, blessed are those who die in Christ. Heaven awaits, whether we die or are "caught up in the air" at Christ's second coming.

We should sing for heaven; long for that glorious place; rejoice because some day we will be there. We ought to be homesick and at the same time not weary in doing the will of Christ and being a blessing to others.

Let all saints, especially you who are sorrowing, know that heaven is a place of consolation. "There is no sorrow on earth which cannot be comforted in heaven."

Heaven and Labour

In dying, a Christian not only gains consolation in heaven, he also receives marvellous rest from his labours. So let us not complain that we have to toil on this earth. The Lord Jesus Christ declared, "I must work the works of Him that sent me, while it is day" (John 9: 4). Paul says that he is not less than the other apostles, but as a minister of Christ, he laboured the more (2 Cor. 11: 23; Acts 20: 31; 2 Cor. 1: 8).

Actually, the apostle all but overworked himself (2 Cor. 1: 8). It is shameful for a Christian to be lazy. The fields are white already for harvest. Therefore we should work hard and, praise be to God, there is rest in heaven. For the Christian, heaven means a pleasant, joyous rest. This is part of our blessing which the Holy Scriptures promise to those who die in Christ (Rev. 14: 13). How wonderful it must be for the Christian in heaven to leave aside all his cares and burdens, and to know that his works follow him.

Young people seem to think that they will never get old. They crave for struggle and challenge. But later on one begins to feel tired; not really tired *of* work, but *in* the work; and the struggle can get difficult. Even preachers of the gospel would at times like to be able to sit under the shadow of some green tree in the midst of a magnificent garden or beside the beach, or simply sit at home with the family and rest. But it rarely happens. For many preachers, as well as for many other Christians who work diligently for the Lord, the time of rest and fellowship at home almost never comes. I think it will be so wonderful for the tired Christian when he can sit at the side of the river of life, under the shadow of the tree of life. What a glorious day of rest that will be!

In this world the sincere Christian father must care for his family. Clothes must be bought, food provided, rent paid, etc. The Christian mother also is busy night and day. There are no forty-hour weeks for her. She has no time to be sick, to sit down, read and rest. But let all Christians who are tired and worn rejoice in the comforting fact that one day they will rest from their work. Rest is part of the wonderful gain of those who die in the Lord.

Our arduous toil is part of the judgment on this world because of sin. Thorns and weeds in the fields, suffering and birth pains, all these and similar things are the result of sin. But one day God will reach out His hand for His children and take them from this world. Then every labour will be finished and we will enter into His everlasting rest (Heb. 4: 1–11). For the souls "under the altar in heaven", the apostle John says: "they should rest yet for a little season" (Rev. 6: 11).

The Reward of Heaven

Furthermore, to die in Christ means to gain eternal recompense. One of the reasons why it is so blessed for a man to die in Christ is that he immediately steps into the fruit of all his labour. He can then rejoice in the riches he has gathered in heaven. This is well stated by the apostle Paul in 2 Timothy 4: 6–8: "For I am already being offered, and the time of my departure is come. I have fought the good fight, I have finished the course, I have kept the faith: henceforth there is laid up for me the crown of righteousness, which the Lord, the righteous judge, shall give to me at that day; and not to me only, but also to all them that have loved his appearing."

It is clear in the Word of God that one portion of the reward of the Christian will be his participation in the government of Christ. When the Lord comes in His glory and the bodies of the saints are resurrected, then the twelve apostles will sit on twelve thrones and will judge the twelve tribes of Israel. Oh, to hear the Lord Jesus say on that day: "Well, done, thou good servant: because thou hast been faithful in very little, have much" (Luke 19: 17).

The apostle Paul well knew that when a person leaves this earth, he will be with Christ in unspeakable joy, seeing those come home whom he has brought to faith in Christ. His works will follow him. Therefore, it is appropriate to ask the question; what works will follow you and me? Remember what the prophet Daniel said? He stated, "they that be wise shall shine as the brightness of the firmament" (12: 3).

How wonderful to be a Christian and to serve God faithfully! We may say for certain that eternal glory and reward await the Christian. Therefore, death has no fears. It is an entrée into the glories of God. Are you ready for that day? Amen!

Arise ye, and depart

Pastor Angeloff

Micah 2: 10

Arise and go, for this is no place to rest;
because of uncleanness that destroys with a grievous
destruction.

The prophet Micah lived and prophesied during a time of moral and spiritual decline, in the midst of a people who were fast moving towards captivity and destruction. He denounced with gloomy words his time and declared like the prophet Amos (5: 13) and the apostle Paul (Eph. 5: 16) that "the time is wicked". The corruption was such, that the prophet says: "If a man walking in the spirit and falsehood do lie, saying, I will prophesy unto thee of wine and of strong drink; he shall even be the prophet of this people" (Mic. 2: 11). The faithful and sincere preachers were forbidden to preach.

Since that time the hands of the clock have turned. And they have come full circle and now point to the same hour and again people like to listen to vain things and lies, and refuse to listen to the word of God. Against the background of sin and corruption in his day the prophet Micah says to Israel: "Arise ye, and depart; for this is not your rest: because it is polluted, it shall destroy you, even with a sore destruction" (2: 10). This is not an exhortation to run somewhere into a secure place, but a warning that they will be brought into captivity.

Now, as I have said, the clock hands have turned and humanity is living in similar times as in the day of Micah. Thus the Word of God declares for today as well: "Arise ye, and depart; for this is not your rest." This is not the place nor the time to fortify one's position, because we are only passing through the world. This world is not our heritage. Our permanent citizenship is not

166

in this earth, it is in heaven. We have no permanent city for we
look for a city "which has foundations, whose builder and maker
is God". Our place in this world is *with* Christ, *outside* the camp,
where we carry His reproach, because we are not of the world.
He took us out of the world, and as He is so are we in this world.

This World Is Not Our Home

No Christian should be attached to this world as if he was going
to live here forever. We must "take heed to yourselves, least at
any time your hearts be overcharged with . . . cares of this life,
and so that day come upon you unawares" (Luke 21: 34). The
Lord tells us again, "If any man comes to me, and hates not
his father, and mother, and wife, and children, and brethren,
and sisters, yea, and his own life also, he cannot be my disciple".
These words seem very harsh, but their meaning is that no earthly
ties should make us less "heavenly". They do not mean that we
should not love our dear ones less, but that we should love Him
more.

The apostle Paul wrote: "But this I say, brethren, the time is
short; it remaineth, that both they that have wives be as though
they had none; and they that weep, as though they wept not;
and they that rejoice, as though they rejoiced not; and they that
buy, as though they possessed not; and they that use this world, as
not abusing it; for the fashion of this world passeth away" (1 Cor.
7: 29–31). This means that we should not give ourselves to earthly
cares, sorrows, joys, nor to our temporary possessions, because
the time is short and the present condition of this world is passing (1 John 2: 17). Of course, we are not to hide like the prover-
bial hermits did in the rocks and caves to escape the world. But at
the same time we must not give ourselves entirely to the tran-
sitory, because we are eternal. God created us such.

A wealthy woman once asked her servant, "Tell me, how is it
that you are always happy? Does nothing disturb you?" She
answered: "My lady, I wear this world like a 'wide garment'."
Yes, the cares of this world should be carried lightly, not pressed
closely to our spirits; as a wide garment. There is no peace for
the child of God in *this world*. But our peace is in Christ, and
we can have the peace of Christ while still in the world. In the
midst of the chaos and clamour of arms, the Christian can be

in peace in the world. This is the wonderful paradox of the Christian experience.

Blessed is the man who, being in the body, yet lives out his lifestyle in heavenly places. He does not abuse this world. The things he possesses do not possess him. They are only means for his sustenance; "having food and raiment", he is satisfied. That is why his prayer is, "Remove far from me vanity and lies: give me neither poverty nor riches; feed me with food convenient for me: lest I be full, and deny thee and say, Who is the Lord? or lest I be poor, and steal, and take the name of my God in vain" (Proverbs 30: 8, 9). He does not get involved in this world in order that he may please Him who has chosen him to be his soldier. He does not love the world or what is in this world. He believes that the Lord will soon come, and for this reason his meekness is known to everybody. He does not take pride in poverty, nor does he live in luxury. He knows that humility consists not in underestimating oneself, but simply in thinking *nothing* of oneself. He does not hide from the world, but is hidden in Christ while moving on in this world. He is not a citizen of this world travelling to heaven, but on the contrary, he is a citizen of heaven living on this earth, longing for his real home. He knows that for the children of God there is an eternal rest, and a heart truly rests only there.

A Sensible Word

This text is not only a warning for the Christian, it is a word of good, practical advice. The heart of man, whether he is a saint or a sinner, finds no rest and peace in the world. Peace is not bought with money, nor can education procure it, nor fame acquire it. Pleasures chase it away, they certainly do not create it. This world is not our permanent home; therefore, how unwise is the man who covers his nest with worldly feathers and makes his permanent residence here. One day he will hear the cruel voice of death saying, "Arise ye, and depart. It is time for you to leave, you cannot stay here any longer." How can a man be rooted in this world, while he is constantly moving towards eternity?

The foolish rich man in Luke 12: 16–21 said to himself, "Soul, thou hast much goods laid up for many years; take thine ease, eat, drink, and be merry." But God said unto him, "Thou fool, this night thy soul shall be required of thee." The Lord knows our time much better than we know it. Abraham told the rich man, "Son remember that thou in thy lifetime receivedst thy good things . . . but now . . ." (Luke 16: 25). The young man who could not follow Jesus because of his love of wealth went away sorrowful for he had "great possessions" (Matt. 19: 22). Yet in reality, he had nothing, because in not gaining Christ he lost everything. When the disciples came back from their missionary journey, the Lord told them, "When I sent you without purse, and scrip, and shoes, lacked ye any thing?" And they said, "Nothing" (Luke 22: 35). The rich young man seemingly had everything. He lacked nothing in this world. Yet he missed everything. The only permanent, sure wealth in this world is to have Christ as one's own Saviour. And on the contrary, the only real poverty is to be without Christ, without the Saviour.

The Word of God tells us that "The grass withereth, the flower fadeth" (Isaiah 40: 7), and "so also shall the rich man fade away in his ways" (James 1: 11). "The earth mourneth and fadeth away, the world languishes and fadeth away" (Isaiah 24: 4). But there are two things which never fade away:

1. An "inheritance incorruptible . . . and that fadeth not away" (1 Peter 1: 4).
2. "A crown of glory that fadeth not away" (1 Peter 5: 4).

Please note that the one is an inheritance. For an inheritance we do not labour, it is a gift from God which we receive by faith in Jesus Christ. The rich young man was quite confused in his ideas. "And behold, one came and said to him, Good Master, what good thing shall I do, that I may have eternal life?" (Matt. 19: 16). We do not labour in order to obtain eternal life. But for a reward in heaven we labour: "Know ye not that they which run in a race run all, but one receiveth the prize? So run, that you may obtain" (1 Cor. 9: 24). There we have the most sensible business transaction in the world: instead of labouring for titles and things which fade away and perish, why not gather riches in heaven "where neither moth nor rust doth corrupt, and where thieves do not break through nor steal" (Matt. 6:20)?

The psalmist says, "In the Lord put I my trust: how say ye to my soul, Flee as a bird to your mountain?" (Ps. 11: 1). The world says, "Forget your misery and turn to pleasure; drink, go here and there. And if nothing gives you pleasure, put an end to your life." But this is not the way to get out of trouble. The Christian, however, knows that there is no place in the world where one can hide. Thus he does not expect anything else from the world but sorrow (John 16: 33). He trusts in the Lord and in time of need finds refuge in the Rock which is sufficient for him (Ps. 61: 2).

How Is It With You?

Do you have restless nights, spending long hours awake thinking how to pay your debts, or how to make both ends meet for the family, how to pay the taxes, or a thousand other things? Perhaps in this way God is trying to teach you to lay up treasure in heaven, not on earth. Have you been ill with pain passing like lightning through your body? Perhaps He wants you to learn that "our light affliction which is but for a moment, worketh for us a far more exceeding and eternal weight of glory" (2 Cor. 4: 17).

Most of the worldly people, the unbelievers, cannot endure hardships, suffering and sorrow. They try to stifle them in pleasures and drown the grief in alcohol. But when all these prove of no help, what can they do? Where can they turn? There is, however, a way to "get up and go out" of this world even while you are in the midst of it. A man can be a citizen of Heaven while he is a pilgrim on this earth. How? By being born into the heavenly family through a childlike faith in Christ.

The plea is to get up and go to Golgotha. We are told that in days past, when the prairies burned, the most efficient way to combat the fire was to burn large areas of the dry grass at a great distance from the fire, and when the fire reached those areas, as there was nothing left to burn, the fire died away.

There is a place in this world where the fire of God's wrath has already passed. And with wrath gone, peace can be found. This place is Golgotha. Two thousand years ago sin and Satan raged terribly around the crucified Saviour; Jesus cried with a loud voice: "My God, my God, why hast thou forsaken me?" But it was right there that sin and Satan were defeated and judged. Now peace pervades Calvary. So get up *now* and go to that holy place, and you will be forever secure from God's wrath because there is no judgment – only peace – for those who are in Jesus Christ.   Amen!

170

Where is Zebedee?

Pastor Angeloff

Mark 1: 16–22

*And passing along by the Sea of Galilee, he saw
Simon and Andrew the brother of Simon casting a
net in the sea; for they were fishermen. And Jesus
said to them, "Follow me and I will make you
become fishers of men." And immediately they left
their nets and followed him. And going on a little
farther, he saw James the son of Zebedee and John
his brother, who were in their boat mending the
nets. And immediately he called them; and they left
their father Zebedee in the boat with the hired
servants, and followed him.*

*And they went into Capernaum; and immediately
on the sabbath he entered the synagogue and
taught. And they were astonished at his teaching,
for he taught them as one who had authority, and
not as the scribes.*

This Scripture text provides the first and last mention of Zebedee,
the father of James and John. Still, a very important lesson can
be learned from him though he be rather obscure. We read in
the Bible that his sons became followers of Christ. They left their
father; they left the boat and the hired servants; they left *everything* and followed Jesus.

The Sons of Zebedee

In the Gospels we read a great deal about the sons of Zebedee.
The first apostle to be martyred was James the son of Zebedee.
John his brother was a writer. He wrote what I consider the most

171

captivating book in all literature; the Gospel of John. These sons of Zebedee were at the mountain of Transfiguration. They were at Calvary when Jesus died. Our Lord committed His mother into the care of John. This same John was the one who outran Peter and arrived first at the empty tomb, and believed. The sons of Zebedee were together with the other disciples at the shore of the lake of Galilee on that wonderful morning when the Resurrected Christ asked them if they had any food and then invited them to share His meal (John 21: 1–14). John was the first to recognize Christ and said to Peter: "It is the Lord." Simply put, the sons of Zebedee followed Christ and were *always* with Him.

But what about Zebedee? This question has a note of sadness in it. The Bible merely states his sons left him in the boat mending his nets with the servants. Perhaps something like this occurred; Zebedee was busy mending nets and he said,

"Good-bye my sons! "

"Father, come with us," they pleaded. "Jesus has so much to offer."

"Sons, I am very busy; I cannot leave my work."

Perhaps even the Lord said, "Zebedee, come with me."

"I am very busy. The nets are torn and they must be mended."

What about his wife? Well, she was with Christ. The Word of God speaks about her as being the mother of the children of Zebedee. Sometimes she was a bit impertinent, another time even a little silly. But this is understandable, a mother will do almost anything on behalf of her children. Like any other mother would have done, she asked that her two sons might have the first place in the Kingdom of God. But she was honest. She did not conceal anything. She openly told Christ what was her desire. And, although she did not have all the spiritual insight that might be desired, still among the pitiless crowd around the cross on which Christ was crucified you find the sons of Zebedee with their mother. She was indeed present, and that is what matters.

Where Is Zebedee?

But where is Zebedee? He is busy, mending nets while his boat drifts on the waves of the sea. He does not lift up his eyes, nor does he hear anything. He sees only the immediate. He just stays on the shore mending nets.

172

Of course, Zebedee had some commendable features in his character. He did not forbid his wife to follow Christ; he did not scold her nor frown. Some men obstinately stand in their family's way. Zebedee was not that type of man. He never hindered his wife or sons from following Christ. But he was not interested himself. He was merely passive about it all.

Now think how much Zebedee lost by his indifference. But, you ask, is it sinful or unrighteous for a man to mend nets? Not at all! Nets must be mended if you want to catch fish. Is it evil to go fishing? Of course not! A man must fish, otherwise people will go hungry. Is it bad to have a boat? No! What then was wrong with Zebedee? The issue is, he would not go with Christ. His wife followed Christ, his sons too, but he preferred to stay with the hired servants and mend the nets. Let us see what Zebedee missed and lost in not following Christ:

What Zebedee Missed

1. *First, Zebedee missed the companionship of Christ.* Suppose you had the opportunity of choosing between Christ and another of the world's famous men. I think I would not be wrong in saying that most of us would have preferred to see Christ. (One day, be sure, everybody on this earth will see Him in judgment.) But Zebedee deliberately failed to follow Christ when he had his chance. Why? The Word of God gives the reason. Because he was too busy with his nets. Too busy to see Christ's smile. Too busy to see the revelation of the Son of God.

"Why, Zebedee? Why did you not follow this holy One from God?"

No other reason, simply too busy!

What a vast difference there is between Zebedee and Zacchaeus (see Luke 19) who closed his office without minding the people, ran and climbed up a sycamore tree in order to see Christ. It was to Zacchaeus that the Lord declared, "Salvation has come to this home." I would prefer a thousand times over to be as Zacchaeus instead of as Zebedee. O Zebedee, will you not come to know Christ; why lose your life in mending nets? And, remember, there is a bit of Zebedee in us all.

2. *Zebedee failed to hear Christ.* Everbody who has read Charles Dickens' *David Copperfield* has enjoyed the novel. The

173

author makes his heroes live and we listen to their words avidly while we are reading the book. But what is that or any great literary work in comparison with the word of Christ? Would you not rather hear Him when He prays, when He teaches, when He ministers to people? Would you not like to hear the remarkable sermon on the mount? This was indeed a wonderful message, and how I would have loved to have heard the sermon at the well near Sychar in Samaria. Sermons preached to lonely or fallen sinners, or to people with broken hearts – these thrill me. Zebedee could have heard these marvellous sermons, but he did not. Why? Because he preferred to mend nets instead of following Christ. Poor Zebedee!

3. *Zebedee never saw Christ do miracles of grace.* Would you not like to have seen Christ walking along the desert paths and there suddenly come upon a leper, a man rejected by the world? Jesus approaches him and the leper cries out, "Unclean! Unclean!" He covers his face with his hands, thinking that Christ will turn away from him; but instead Christ goes right up to him and touches him.

Would you not like to have seen that? In principle, you can see it today. But you must leave your torn nets and come to Christ. If you do, He will touch you with His pierced hand and your sinful heart will be purified and renewed as the flesh of the leper in the desert.

Would you not like to have been in Bethany near Jerusalem when Jesus came to the home of the two sisters Martha and Mary – four days after the death of their beloved brother? Would you not like to have been at the tomb and to have heard Jesus say, "Lazarus, come forth!"?

"Zebedee, where are you?"

"I am in a hurry, my nets are terribly torn!"

4. *Zebedee failed to see the Cross.* Probably all of us would like to see the sphinx in Egypt, one of the seven wonders of the ancient world. Or who would not like to see some of the latest discoveries of human genius? But above all these things, our greatest need is to see Calvary's Cross and Christ crucified upon that tree for you and me and the whole sinful world.

"But, Zebedee, what are you doing? Mending your nets still? Don't you see Golgatha?"

"I don't know. I am too busy."

Zebedee, there on the Cross is Christ; a ransom for men's sins. That is why the earth is shaking and the waters of Galilee are raging. For a moment Zebedee lifts up his eyes, but then he merely says, "The storm is coming, set the sails." And poor Zebedee does not know that the sea is raging on account of Christ's death. What a tragedy!

5. *Zebedee failed to see the empty tomb.* What a glorious day that first resurrection morn must have been. I would have sacrificed all in order to see the empty tomb as Peter and John did on the resurrection morning. Don't you pity Zebedee that he missed that opportunity? Life does not consist in eating and drinking alone. There is more to life than mending nets.

I bewail Zebedee, but in all sincerity there are many Zebedees around us for whom we should cry.

"Oh Zebedee, what are you doing? Your wife and children are safe in Christ; and you, where are you?"

"But you don't understand. I am a very busy man."

Why Be So Concerned?

And some "up to date" Zebedees have no greater excuse than he. But why should Zebedee be so concerned about spiritual things, like following Christ? If for no other reason, that he is the head of the family. When a man marries, he gives not only his name to his family, but his influence as well. What a pity for the husband and father who has no spiritual influence or impact in his home. In those days the father was the priest in the home. And Zebedee missed it all. He cheated himself, and almost cheated his family, but for the grace of Christ.

But where are you, you contemporary Zebedee? My heart is broken for you, my friend, neighbour and citizen. Why are you not following Christ, Zebedee? Why don't you pray? Why don't you turn to Christ? Why do you not lead your family to Jesus? O Lord, call Zebedee this day. Call him to come to Christ. Call him to come to Thee with his wife and children. This is my prayer and plea for you all. Amen!

Sermons from
CZECHOSLOVAKIA

Stanislav Svec

The Reverend Stanislav Svec was born on November 14, 1925 in Moravia, Czechoslovakia; in the little village of Vsetim. His parents were devoted Christians, and his father was a Baptist lay preacher. He is one of six children, all of whom are believers.

Stanislav Svec was converted at the age of sixteen during an evangelistic campaign held in his home church. After the second world war, he felt the call to the ministry. He studied engineering at the University of Prague, and then from 1946 to 1950, after his call to preach the gospel, he studied at the Baptist Seminary in Prague. He also took special study at Spurgeon's Theological College in London, England.

He served as pastor of the Second Baptist Church of Prague for some years. Being a most successful minister he was called to the First Baptist Church of Prague and elected to the post of General Secretary of the Baptist Union of Czechoslovakia. It is now as pastor and General Secretary that he faithfully serves Christ.

Abide with us !

Stanislav Svec

Luke 24: 13–33

*That very day two of them were going to a village
named Emmaus, about seven miles from Jerusalem,
and talking with each other about all these things
that had happened. While they were talking and
discussing together, Jesus himself drew near and
went with them. But their eyes were kept from
recognizing him. And he said to them, "What is this
conversation which you are holding with each other
as you walk?" And they stood still, looking sad.
Then one of them, named Cleopas, answered him,
"Are you the only visitor to Jerusalem who does not
know the things that have happened there in these
days?" And he said to them, "What things?" And
they said to him, "Concerning Jesus of Nazareth,
who was a prophet mighty in deed and word before
God and all the people, and how our chief priests
and rulers delivered him up to be condemned to
death, and crucified him. But we had hoped that
he was the one to redeem Israel. Yes, and besides
all this, it is now the third day since this happened.
Moreover, some women of our company amazed
us. They were at the tomb early in the morning
and did not find his body; and they came back
saying that they had even seen a vision of angels,
who said that he was alive. Some of those who were
with us went to the tomb, and found it just as the
women had said; but him they did not see." And he
said to them, "O foolish men, and slow of heart to
believe all that the prophets have spoken! Was it
not necessary that the Christ should suffer these
things and enter into his glory?" And beginning with*

*Moses and all the prophets, he interpreted to them
in all the scriptures the things concerning himself.
So they drew near to the village to which they
were going. He appeared to be going further, but
they constrained him, saying, "Stay with us, for it is
toward evening and the day is now far spent."
So he went in to stay with them. When he was at
table with them, he took the bread and blessed, and
broke it, and gave it to them. And their eyes were
opened and they recognized him; and he vanished
out of their sight. They said to each other, "Did not
our hearts burn within us while he talked to us on
the road, while he opened to us the scriptures?"
And they rose that same hour and returned to
Jerusalem; and they found the eleven gathered
together and those who were with them.*

The passage of Scripture that forms our text is a beautiful story; we all know and understand it well, because it describes so perfectly our own human situation. You see, it is you and I – all of us – who so often go through life disappointed, tired and heartbroken. Moreover, we do not travel this way only occasionally, we go down that road often. Yes, we travel that route again and again. It is in our lot in life – at least so it would seem!

Yet in the face of life's difficulties and perplexities, we have our good and kindly Lord who never leaves us or forsakes us. He goes with us, even in the worst of circumstances. Once I remember that I had a very difficult and unpleasant duty. My own human strength forsook me and I was outright frightened. But then as I set out on the way to try and settle the matter, a brother from our church saw me in the road. He crossed over to me, took my hand and said, "My brother, I always pray when walking along the road. Just now I have been praying for you!" I took it as a clear assurance that I was not going alone, that I had no need to fear, for the Lord Jesus was with me.

Sometimes the Lord approaches us through people; sometimes He approaches us in His Word. We read our Bible and its words suddenly have a new, deep, personal meaning which we never

181

noticed before. Another time the Lord may speak to us through a hymn, or through the gift of bread we eat. But however He comes to us, we get new strength to face life's problems. Regardless of how trying things may seem, one thing is certain, the Lord Jesus comes into our world of experience and takes our burdens upon Himself. He goes with us to release us from our fears and sorrows and anxieties.

A Christian Responsibility

But let us apply the story in our text in a different manner. We are not to be preoccupied only with our worries. Does not our Master challenge us by means of this recorded event in another area of Christian experience? Remember, He said, "As the Father has sent me, even so I send you" (John 20: 21). Does our Lord not send us to go and weep over the crushed hopes of others, that is, to identify with other people who are weeping, disappointed, and despondent? But not merely to weep with them, but to tell them about Jesus who is alive, who loves them, in whom there is the hope of eternal life! Surely that is our task.

Many Christians in many parts of the world as well as Czechoslovakian believers, live in countries with many old Christian traditions. However, there are multitudes of people in all our nations that do not truly believe in the Lord Jesus Christ. According to official statistics, forty per cent of the population of my country are non-believers. Still, they are always reminded of the existence of God and of His Son Jesus Christ. Every day they go past churches full of worshippers; they see many crosses – symbols of the Divine Love; they can read Christian slogans in many places; they know of Christian days which they too, observe – even Sunday, the Lord's day. Of course, it often happens that these people, when in trouble, remember God and call on Him for help. But what they lack is Jesus Christ and a true knowledge of His glorious salvation. I dare say that many of the so-called "believers" actually do not have Jesus Christ in any true dynamic way at all. Consequently, they do not have genuine peace or joy in their souls. They have hours of loneliness, disappointment, despondency, despair, and do not know where to seek for help. If all these people were

182

quite suddenly called upon to face death – say the loss of a beloved one, or their own death – then it would become obvious how helpless and miserable they are. In spite of all our technological advance and materialism that man is so proud of, in spite of all human efforts, success, and enjoyment, how poor man appears in the face of death. He, without Christ, lacks everything of lasting value that can help him overcome the storms of his life; yes, to overcome death and to enable him to reach eternal life!

The Ultimate Answer

The two disciples on their way to Emmaus thought they knew quite well their need; they imagined they lacked Jesus, their Master! They had known Him as the Lord; some of their brethren even confessed Him to be the Son of God. They had joined Him, and they set all their hopes upon Him. But quite unexpectedly He was taken away from them, crucified, killed. This was the reason of their grief, and they knew it.

However, most people rarely realize what is the real reason for their fears and trouble. They are worried, exhausted, anxious – and they usually attribute it to a number of various reasons. They talk about their nerves, their overwork and innumerable other "causes". But they do not often admit that what they really do not have is the peace of God. They try to allay their troubles in a multiplicity of ways, but all in vain. One would think they should know quite well that human remedies for suffering souls are entirely ineffective, because they simply cannot do away with the real reason of the trouble. There is only one Healer and only one Remedy: Jesus Christ. He alone can effect reconciliation of the person with God through His blood. And, because we who are Christians know this, we are to go and find those suffering people and lead them to Jesus Christ.

True, this is not easy. Most people do not know Jesus Christ at all, and they wonder what He could do for them. They know nothing of His love, of His readiness to forgive their sins, and of His power to help them in their trouble. They do not recognize Him when He approaches them; they seemingly cannot hear His voice speaking to them. They do not understand. But still – and this is a very old and well known experience – they do feel better when they are in touch with anything or anyone that reminds them of Christ. They are much like the disciples on their way to Emmaus: though they did not recognize their Master, their hearts "burned within them".

During the last war, I was taken along with a number of my school-chums to a labour camp in Nazi Germany. All my friends knew that I was a Christian, and sometimes they mocked me, good-naturedly. But when the air raids came and we were in danger and fear, they all tried to be close to me as if I could make them safer. So it is! People do mock, but still they seek in times of trouble those who are the people of God. Somehow they sense God's people can be trusted and needn't be feared; it is good to be with them, they feel.

Yet at times, even the people of God may make the same mistake, that is, they mistake God's real ways; "we trusted that it had been he which should have redeemed Israel!" Redeem Israel from Roman supremacy! That was what the Emmaus Road disciples expected Christ to do. They were looking for a material kingdom, and in that they were sadly disappointed. All people that were "seeking their own" – mere material values – were disappointed by Jesus Christ. Thus, the mother of John and James who begged the Lord to let her sons sit one on his right hand and the other on the left in His Kingdom; or Simon in Samaria who offered money to the apostles for the gift of the Holy Ghost; everyone who expected Christ to grant him profit, success, a life of comfort and prosperity, courted disappointment. The same is true today. If people expect Christ to transform secular "kingdoms" and bring about some sort of "Christian state", they will miss what Christ is doing in this world.

The Kingdom Is Spiritual

What Jesus has brought is not of this world. True, His Kingdom has come into this world and is meant for the people of this world, but it surpasses and outlasts the temporal. Jesus has come to reconcile man with God; to cleanse man's heart and mind; to give him eternal and abundant life. This is the nature of His Kingdom. And this too is the heart of the commission of His disciples and witnesses: they are to preach the forgiveness of sins through the faith in Jesus Christ. They are to preach eternal life. And what is the nature of this eternal life? Well, it is simply everyday life, made beautiful by the presence of God; aimed at heavenly, not secular, values. Therefore, it is a joyful and happy life, a full and everlasting life that overcomes death and hell. This is what we are to announce. What a glorious message!

However, we must never forget that we are not merely to talk about these things. Remember, when the Lord Jesus was talking to His disciples on the way to Emmaus, they did not recognize Him. It was not His talk *alone* that led to the recognition, but His deed in the breaking of bread. Thus, we too come to know our Lord best from His deed, that is, His impact on our human situations and needs.

Deeds are Vital

So we are committed to preach the Lord Jesus, to help people know Him and understand Him. But as much as we may talk and preach, it will do little good if our deeds do not undergird our witness. Words must be followed by action; by life. Or perhaps the action should actually precede our words: people must usually *see* our faith, our devotion, our obedience before they will believe. They normally must see us as fully devoted to our Lord at work and rest, always and everywhere; in our family life, in our fellowship at church – everything we do is to witness to the love of God and the power of His Spirit if they are to be impressed by our words.

"Abide with us, for it is toward evening . . ." – that is what the disciples were asking for, though they had not recognized who was with them. This is always the desire of man: to have someone with them – someone whom they need not fear, someone to help and understand.

The Christian's Responsibility

Now, it is *you*, Christian friend, who are sent to identify with your neighbour, to stay with him as it were, to be his support. *You* are now in the place of Jesus Christ, for you are His follower and in you the Lord wants to "stay" with people who need Him. Oh, stay with those who are in want; make them feel your

185

concern, your love. Serve them; pray for them.

Yes, we sometimes let people feel that we are interested in them, that we like them, and we may even pray for someone here and there. But people want us to "abide" with them – to stay, not to leave as our whims may choose. And that is why the Lord sends us to them. It is not easy, this task of self-giving, but this very act is the mark of our discipleship; of our adherence to Jesus Christ.

The Lord wants to abide with us, and through us with them who need Him. Open your heart to Him, and let Him use you in His service! That is how the world will come to know Him. Amen!